T0090443

ROCKY MOUNTAIN TALES

Wit and Wisdom of the Wild West

Arlene Pervin

Edited by Brian Conrad

Order this book online at www.trafford.com
or email orders@trafford.com

Most Trafford titles are also available at major online book retailers.

Printed in Victoria, BC, Canada.

ISBN: 978-1-4269-3170-3 (sc)
ISBN: 978-1-4269-3171-0 (eb)

*Our mission is to efficiently provide the world's finest, most comprehensive book publishing
service, enabling every author to experience success. To find out how to publish your
book, your way, and have it available worldwide, visit us online at www.trafford.com*

Trafford rev. 05/04/2010

 www.trafford.com

North America & international
toll-free: 1 888 232 4444 (USA & Canada)
phone: 250 383 6864 ♦ fax: 812 355 4082

In Memory of

Israel and Evelyn Pervin
Who gave me their hearts
And my life's foundation

and

To all who dare to follow their dreams

PREFACE

The following stories are of men and women who were boosters of their towns, spoke their minds, cast aside conventions, put their hearts forward and led with their deeds and words. Many of these stories come from newspapers from the 1900s. It was the boom and bust days of the developing West.

As a researcher and editor, I feel the process of extracting these nuggets of history for me is akin to being an octopus extending its tentacles, searching and exploring hidden sources and unknown territory. In that exploratory world, my editorial eye sees something in the words themselves that stands out. It is the voice of the writer of the poem, story, or news editorial that tells not only of time past, but of human circumstance.

Time frames each moment. Words capture intelligence, passion, adventure, and the political drift of a certain time and place. They tell of people who lived, thought, triumphed and despaired. They breathe life into events that happened yesterday or long ago. Words reveal personality, prejudice, political biases, emotional states and social classes, and they can be as cutting as a scalpel or as flowery as a spring bouquet.

The words and cadences in language may be a bit different, having been written a century before, but what comes through is our innate humanness.

Perhaps, this is what I intend for the reader, to appreciate the innate humanness in these stories.

Table of Contents

BACON AND CIVILIZATION

Newspapers in the early 1900s not only contained regional news of the towns' business, but also carried advertisements of upcoming events, ads for local businesses, remedies, jokes and entertaining stories.

It would have been very difficult to fill a small town newspaper with only local news, so editors often filled their papers with additional story items taken from other sources like popular magazines and other newspapers of the day.

These stories provided additional entertainment and interest for their readers and contributed to the overall make–up of the newspaper. Sometimes the author of the story got mentioned and often not. Sometimes it was the work of a clever editor himself, if he was also a gifted writer.

The following story does not mention the author's name but the voice of the writer comes through, and not only provides entertainment but food for thought.

What do the Statue of Liberty and bacon have in common? According to this rasher lover, one wouldn't be there without the other. This testament to "Bacon and Civilization" comes from Banff's *Crag and Canyon* of Feb 18, 1901.

"I have a profound respect for bacon." Remarked a thoughtful citizen at a Calgary café the other day, spearing one of the savory brown slices that garnished his breakfast eggs. "Did it ever occur to you that we are indebted primarily to bacon for the opening up and development and civilization of this great and glorious West. That, without bacon, this grand country, with its thriving cities, its fertile farms, its magnificent mines and its gigantic railroad, telephone and telegraph lines, and all its other wonderful evidences of progress and prosperity—that, without bacon, this superbly flourishing domain would probably be a howling wilderness at the present moment?" The thoughtful citizen paused for breath. "You astonish me," said his friend across the table. "That is because you have never given any subject any attention", he replied. "Bacon has been the chief agency in the development of this country, for the simple reason that it has been the chief food of the pioneer. It was the only kind of meat that was easily portable and would keep for an indefinite period. Freemont's pathfinders carried it; so did the gold hunters of '49, and so did that tremendous army of emigrants and frontiersmen who gradually opened up the unknown region between the Red River and the Pacific coast. The prospectors who toiled up and down the continental divide and located the great mineral resources of the country lived upon bacon and to this day it is the main item in the 'grub stake' of every adventurer who goes into the mountains to seek for ore.

"To sum the matter up, the advance guard of civilization has moved steadfastly westward eating bacon and conquering savage nature, and without that humble article of diet the red man and the bison would still be prowling over the regions where 'pink teas' flourish and culture rules the roost. You must bear in mind, too, that the bacon upon which all these vast achievements are based was not the high-priced, delicately flavored breakfast bacon of a first-class café. It is sterner stuff. It is the strong, dark, greasy bacon of ordinary commerce, that comes in great rough slabs and smells like scorched shoe-leather. At first sight you would turn away in disgust, but as a ration to work on and travel on and fight on, it has no equal in the world. I grant you that the fancy condensed foods they are putting up for the armies now-a days are vastly prettier to look at, and the chemist say they contain ten times the nutriment to the square inch, but let a company of tired, hungry soldiers go into camp after a forced march or a fierce battle, and I will wager horses to horsehair that they throw away all their tinned gimcracks for one rasher of good old-fashioned bacon, hot from the griddle. If I had my way about it I would remove the torch from the up-raised hand of Bartholdi's magnificent statue of Liberty Enlightening the World, and substitute a colossal rasher of bacon. Then it would be truly symbolic of western progress."

OF HOBBIES AND HIGH DIVING ELK

High Diving Elk *Moyie Leader*

Sometimes stories fall into the believe-it or-not category. Although given man's inclination to train wild animals and the outstanding relationships between man and beast, a camera's eye proved that seeing is believing in this story of one man's eccentric hobby. The following story was published in the *Moyie City Leader* of the early 1900's. The grainy, black and white photo of an elk plunging headfirst from a wooden platform tells all. Believe it or not.

"High Diving Elk"
"In conversation the other day, Will J. Barnes of Sioux City, Iowa said:

Some people have an eccentric hobby, others have a hobby that appeals to the general run of beings as sensible and proper. Whatever you may call my hobby, it is one that has taken complete possession of me, and I am proud of the sensation it causes. My hobby is my diving elks, which I claim to be the most wonderful animals in the world. But then perhaps I am prejudiced in their favor, as I educated them and taught them the tricks that are a constant source of wonder and admiration to my friends.

"I was prompted to train the elk because I heard it so frequently stated that it was the dullest animal living. The fact that the undertaking seemed to be one almost impossible to carry through successfully gave additional zest to the task I set for myself, which was to train a team of elks to do the most remarkable thing I could think of that was compatible with the nature of the animal.

"I procured two young elks and began experimenting with them at once. I soon discovered that the elks were smart enough to outwit me on several occasions. My first step was to break them to drive harness. This took nearly a year to do, as I had to gain the animals' confidence and friendship before I could do anything with them.

"I succeeded finally, however, in getting them thoroughly broken into a very pleasant driving team. I got my idea of teaching them to dive by their seeming utter indifference as to what height they jumped from while training. In fact, the very first dive they ever made was from a high bank into the Sioux river, on which occasion I went with them.

"I fixed a short chute on the river bank at first and coaxed them to go into it up about five feet high and jump into the water from that height. After a few months of patient work, I got them to run up the chute of their own free will and jump into the water. As it was the only place from which they could get into the water they began to think it great sport to jump from that height. Then I began to raise the platform, and as the weather was getting too cold in Iowa for comfortable training in the river I took the elks south to New Orleans and kept them in constant training all winter, jumping from a higher elevation each week after I had got them to leap from a height of about twenty feet.

"'Ringlette', seemed by instinct to get the true diving idea of making his plunges headfirst, with front feet extended, and now he always goes head foremost and strikes exactly in the center of the tank, which is sixteen feet square and twelve feet deep.

"The buck elk "Ring" is beginning to dive almost as his brother, and I am sure before the summer is past he will dive head foremost, with feet extended as does 'Ringlette'."

Not only is this story a testament to the fact that people do the darndest things but so can animals.

CHEESE AND WILDCATS

Newspapers in the 1900's carried more than news. They provided entertainment by featuring excerpts of popular books or clever short pieces written by creative editors and writers. Like any good story, the following story probably has some underlying truth to it. But one thing for sure, it provides entertainment. The Queen's English is not portrayed here but rather the southern drawl and words of a western cowboy.

The front page of this issue boasts that it was "Published at the Highest Altitude of any Newspaper in British America." A fine line drawing of Mount Assiniboine graces the upper half of the front page with the by-line of "Mt. Assiniboine-12,560ft. above the sea and never scaled by man." Each issue cost 5 cents or $1.00 a year.

Here is the story published in the *Crag and Canyon*, Vol. 1 No.1 from Banff Hot Springs; Alta., Dec 8,1900

Cheese and Wildcats

"Fergy, the guide, had stuck a knot of balsam pine in the fork of a tree near by and it cast a red and fitful light over the tail gate of a wagon which he mounted on two forked uprights to serve as a table. The other man, seated on an upended grocery box, had eaten his lunch and was doubtingly examining a yellow mass, thin and hard, that lay before him.

"That's cheese," said Fergy standing near.

"Yes?" Said the other man questioningly, "As one interested in scientific research, I am glad to have my doubts removed."

"Yaas," said Fergy, "It's funny, but I never had any luck when there is cheese in camp. I told that gal at the hotel not to put no cheese in with our grub and the fust thing I jam my hand agin when I unpack the box is that thar. Put it in yer pocket and keep it to hit an Injun with. You fellers w'at takes three drinks and then hugs yer enemies an fights yer friends makes me fayteeged. Hit him anywhere atween his knees an his hair an it'll fetch him. The other man said nothing.

"Ain't never had no luck with cheese sence the old man Blandon o'Injyanny come up here. He's a banker when he's at home. Nice ol' man he were, easy an peaceful like, and didn't look more'n half awake at no time. I don't understand how he made his money. Bill Humes told me he were wuth four billion dollars, an he got it from a red- headed teller with a impediment in his speech what kep him from being a liar. Most of his truck which I packed to this very spot, were grub what he brought from home. He were so careful o'it I guest he must a kep it in his bank. They was nothin'but canned goods with writin' on em I couldn't read, never see the likes o' em before, and cheese! He were a conosher bout cheese. Had thirty one, I learnt the names o'some, but not all. This is where the story begins."

"Fust night in camp ol' Blandon took a hatchet and broke open one of his boxes what I had lugged; cut here, and took out a little round can an cut it open with his knife and said: "Fergy, we'll have a little Kom-em-bare." He spread the stuff on some toast an handed it to me, an sir, she were good. We et half the can and left it on the table an went to bed. Long bout 1 o'clock I were woke up by the stranges' sweetest music as ever was heard, an I use ter be a fiddler myself. I laid there an liss'nd till I was broad awake an then I lifted my head and looked. Sitten by the fire that had most died down, his tail curled over his back an a grin on his face lixe the angels wear, were the bigges wild cat I ever see before nor sence. An he were chuck full o' cheese. He were so joyful he hadder sing. I love music, an that were music, but I don't want no wild cats where I am sleepin, so I reached for a chunk to shy at it when Whoosh! It were gone. Fur's it went I could hear them beautifying strains, an if they'll only sing that when I git to heaven, I'll stay till hell freezes over.

"I told Blandon bout it next morning an he looked at me an at the empty cheese can an asked me what my stummic was made outer, and said Kom-em-bare cheese must have a singular effect on the untootered imagnashun. It made me mad. We fisht a little that day, but didn't ketch nothing. He kep lookin at me most o' the time an every leetle while he'n arsk me how big thet cat were, an how many stripes it had, an wether its tail was curled over its back er only curved, an a lot o'dam nonsense like that. I thinks onct I'd give the boat a little twist an let him spatter in twenty feet o' water, but he were an ol' man an they were $2 a day in it.

"That night he went to his treasure ches agin an took out nuther priceless can o' smell and says: 'Fergy, we'll have a little Rokefort;' He spread some on a piece of toast an give it to me an, sir, she were good. We et half the can an then we wrapt it up in a piece o' paper an went to bed. Coulden a been moren 12 o'clock when I heered the song. It seemed to have a disappointed note in it, a sorter sound o' sadness, like I lookt up an theres the cat on its stummick by the fire and singen soft an low. I got on my all fours an cralled over to Blandon en yanked him by the whiskers. Here I says, yer the fust man as ever said that Fergy lied and lived to get away with it. Raise up an look at that cat er I'll chaw yer ear. He raised up keerful like and took one look an throwed a fit. Poore ol' man, it knocked him clean off'n the thwart. I thrun a pail o watter over him and he set up an wiped his whiskers. The cat took one jump that landed him forty feet three inches an as he went he lookt back reproachful like as muchas to say,'give me Kome-em bare-er don't give me nothing. Thet cat were a good deal like some people.

"Next day ol' Blandon were the mildest man you ever see. That night we tried the cat on groo-yare, an we got a immertashun o'four fiddles and a drum playin the Arkansaw Traveller. Next night we give him edum, an he'd a jumped on us if I hadn't pulled a gun an told him to go way."

"Next night ol'Blandon says: 'This is a interesting visitor-o'ours, but I'd rather feed him on gold dollars than on em cheeses, fer my stocks gitten low and Gowd knows where I can git any more in this wilderness. To night, Fergy, I'm goin to make him wush he'd kep the simple appetites o' his childhood. With that he goes to his box an drors out a can an gits to the winnard o' me an chopt the top off. Say, I been in the Chicager stock yards in Augus; I been where the creek had dried up an five thousand ton o' feesh were rottin in the sun, but I gits to the other side o' Blandon an say I haint never smell no smell like that smell. I gits to the other side o' Blandon and say I haint goin to die in no sich disgraceful fashion so longs there a gun'thin ten mile. 'This is Lim-bugger,' says he, an eny livin beein, man er cat, has goter be edicated up to it.' With that he et half o' it an leff the other half settin on the table. Fifteen times he come back afore he could git near nuff the stuff to tackle it. Finally he gritted his teeth an jammed his nose inter the can an pulled it out agin. He reminded me o' a ol' boose fighter wat has to kick his self to make him take a drink in the morning. Wen he got a tast o' thet Lim-bugger in his mouth he turned thirty four hansprings and howled, screemed, barked, yapped, sputtered, miaowed, sobbed, coughed, yelled, spit, swore and'hollered. Ol' Blandon set up an prayed. The last I see o' the cat it rewolvin thro the trees twenty feet above the groun an gitten swifter at every turn."

"Now thet cat, before he struck thet Kom-em bare on the fatil night, were jist a ordinary wildcat, with nothing much the matter with him, but that fall we uster hear him. His nature were ruint by excess, an he started out to git even on us all because thet Injianny man had let him astray. He goter be a rogue and quit sociatin with no other cats and up to this time he never tasted no human blood."

"One day a feller started fer town ter git him a drink cause he were dry. Goin long he took out a big spring knife some body give him and tried to open it. He heered a yowlin behind him and sence he hadn't had the drink yet, he were a leetle scairt. He cut his finger on the blade, an as it bled some, he wiped his hand on a bush an then lit fer town 'sfast as blazes. Long come this here cat and lickt the leaves. That settled it. Next week a little boy wandered out in the bush an hain't never been heard of sence. Next week a little gal wandered away, an she were never heard of sence. Next week a little boy.

"Get along," said the other man, " When were you appointed census enumerator?"

"This run on, said Fergy undisturbed 'till everybody was a huntin that cat, but they never seen no sign o' him. The snow wer on the ground when Baptiste Lacroix come long heddin west. He'd been drunk fer two weeks an when his money were all gone they told him they was a lumber camp up the creek where the could work and get some more. Bap being full, lit out thout a nuther word, an as he come along he was fixin how to git even on the bar-keeper. Cause he were French and not English nor Irish er Scotch, this scheme come to him. He stopt and pulled off his shoe. 'I weel be reevanched', says he, I weel cut off ze large toe an haing eet on de bush. Some tam dey come along a see ze poor toe and say Ah-h! We haf don wrrrong to ze poor Baptiste; he good fellaire af b'all. Ze Frainchmon ees not to be ensolted.' So he slasht off his toe and hung it on a sapling. That cat come long bout half an hour afterwards an et the toe.That toe had in it beer, whiskey, brandy, rum, absinthe, wine and wood alcohol, mostly wood alcohol. One day goin thro the woods I heered the ol' songs soundin out over the silent wastes. They were the same an yit they was a unearthly screech runnin lon o'em. Purty soon I see what were the matter. The cat had the jimjams. Memry was gittin the best o' it. The ol' nights in Blandon's camp were throngen upon it, and it were blendin with its song a desire for all sorts o' cheeses. It ud go all the way down thro Kom-em –bare, roke-fort, groo-yare, edum and so on to limbugger, and then the handspring act ud start. When it got to the limbugger stage I took five shots at it an never teched a hair. Last night I see o' it, it were goin tail fust atween the trees and makin dam good time.

"Now that cat had character and staminy. It got them jimmies and braced right up an quit human blood an cheese an things. I took as much pride in that cat's goodness as if it had been my own chile. They come a feller up here from Chicager, with a bike-soot an long hair an he lugged an ol' buffler gun what somebody give him fer a joke. The caliber o' this gun were 62, an it made a roar like 200 hipnertized bulls. This feller used to float round the river with the buffler gun an one day the cat come down there to git a sup o'water. Remember it hadn't had no blood er cheese er drink fer near a year. Jest plain food an regler hours were good nuff fer it. This feller glanced up an see it, an bein scaret to death he raised the buffler gun an shut his eyes an pulled the trigger. Naturally under them circumstances he blowed the cat's head off. "Now," said Fergy, rising and pointing a gnarled forefinger at his companion, "what's the moril o' that?

"The moral, said the other man, yawning is: Never steel cheese from an Indiana banker."

"It aint," said Fergy, "The moril is: Lake watter aint no good fer nothing cep feesh."

CHARISMA AND THE CONMAN

No matter what the century, there will always be con artists, men and women whom you would never expect to pull the wool over your eyes and sweet talk you into a deal or loan which of course would never be repaid.

This particular con man was talented, sociable, charismatic and entertaining– typical characteristics of the type.

He even fooled his musician friends and the newspaper man, Dave Kay, who told his story. Here is the story printed in an early *Cranbrook Herald* about "Ted Leaward" a talented musician and very charismatic con man.

"Here's a story I have had in mind to tell our readers for some time. It is about one of the most remarkable on the many outstanding musicians with which Cranbrook has been blessed over the past roughly seventy years of its existence as a community. This man was a born leader, the best and most versatile musician I have ever worked with, and a grand person to know.

"As is often the case with extremely talented folks, he has certain weaknesses, and it is on account I have hesitated to tell his story here. To tell it right, I must mention some of these, and to do so just might be construed by an unscrupulous surviving relative as libel. He must long since have passed on to his reward, as this all happened many years ago in my early days in Cranbrook. But to protect myself, and this paper, I am going to call him " Ted Leaward", which was not his real name.

"Having been so intimately associated with him, much of this story will be told from my own personal experience, and I hope our readers will forgive me for that. Anyway here we go:

"For many years I was associated with a great variety of the bands, concert orchestra, dance orchestra, etc., with which

Cranbrook was well blessed in those days, And note—our Marching bands, I just may have something to say about that one of these day too!

"As our story begins here, I was playing at that time with a small four –piece dance orchestra—piano, drums, violin, and myself, saxophone and trombone. A violin at that time was considered almost a "must" in any dance group of consequence. Incidentally, I was the first man in Cranbrook to purchase a saxophone and play it in local musical organizations.

"Anyway we had a big dance lined up to be held in the G.W.V.A. (later Legion) hall which was at that time in what is now the Byng Hotel. About a week before the date, our violinist, who worked in the C.P.R. superintendent's office, was suddenly transferred elsewhere, and there we were without a violin player. What to do? We just HAD to get one, but where? The remaining three of us held a council of war to try and find a solution. Finally, our piano player, the late W.D.(Bill) Smith, told us he had been out on a C.P.R. work train at Kitchener a short while before. One evening there had been a sort of lumberjack stag dance in the camp nearby, and Bill as so often happened, had been joed to play the piano for them.

"During the evening, "a drunken bull cook" from one of the lumber camps came up with a violin under his arm and asked if he might join in. Bill told him to go ahead, figuring if he was too bad he could probably drown him out with the piano, along with the considerable stamping and racket of heavy boots and general noise coming from the dance floor. However, almost right away, Bill realized "Ted" for that was who it was, was an outstanding musician, and as our William told us, he could "just make that fiddle talk".

"Well, we realized we were taking a terrific chance, but we were desperate, so asked Bill to contact this man and see if he would play this dance with us. In a short time back came the word, "Yes, he would come.""

"Came the night of the dance. We entered the hall with our fingers crossed and our hearts in our mouths. We were met by a rather short stocky man with iron-grey hair, immaculately dressed in a blue serge suit (which was quite the "in thing", in those days) white shirt, collar and tie, and strictly sober. He gave us each a warm handshake, and said: ' Well boys, it would have been nice if we could have had a practice first, but I'm sure we'll get along fine anyway." And how we did!

"From the very first tune, we knew we had a Real musician, and it was not long before the crowd on the dance floor realized it too! He just took over our little group, like the born leader he was, and pretty soon he had us doing things we never knew we could do. And the crowd just ate it up, demanding encore after encore. Part way through the evening he asked me if he could try out my trombone, and soon a glorious mellow tone came pouring out of that old horn of mine, such as it had never known, For the rest of the evening I was almost ashamed to play it again. "We were the hit of the evening, and the year, and from then on we could take our pick of the many dances put on in Cranbrook at that time, Ted Leawards was the talk of the town, Pretty soon he was playing violin solos at public gatherings of all sorts, with one of the leading social ladies of the city playing his accompaniments.

"His next move was to organize a 35-piece concert orchestra. And he was just as good a conductor as he was a player. He was then offered and accepted leadership of the city band, as he could play and demonstrate just about all of the band instruments, and so understood the problems of the players, he soon brought that organization up to a high standard.

"Not content with all this, a choral group was organized, followed by a Glee Club composed of plucked-string instruments, guitars, mandolins, and banjoes. Then a musical association was formed to consolidate all these groups, and that winter some very fine concerts were put on with the different organizations all taking part, to provide some splendid and varied programs, and all through this period I never knew Ted to touch liquor of any kind.

"About this time his wife came to join him and they took up quarters in an apartment above one of the stores on Baker Street, Here he gave music lessons, and soon had a large class of students. I, along with a few other close friends, was invited up on various occasions for a snack following a band or orchestra practice session, and of course met his wife—a stout, motherly type matron. He always called her "mama" (with the accent on the first syllable), and she seemed to adore her Ted, and sure could serve up a delicious cup of coffee and what went with it, in a short time.

"And so the winter went by, with Ted riding the crest of popularity wave such as few men ever enjoyed in our fair city. He had ability to burn, and a delightful personality along with it. He could bawl a player out during a practice for making a mistake, pick him out among all the other players, tell him what note he played, and what he should have played, then give him a friendly grin, which took all the sting out of it. But you didn't forget next time.

"Came spring and a big outside memorial unveiling ceremony planned for a certain Sunday. Of course the choral group would lead the singing and the band accompany them. And of course, Ted would conduct the combined groups.

"The week previous "Mama" had to go to Spokane for a serious operation. Two days before the unveiling ceremony, Ted received a telegram from Spokane saying his wife had died on the operating table. I saw the message myself, along with many others. All were much concerned, expressed their sympathy, and wondered about the big "do" on the Sunday.

"However, Ted told us he was an old showman, and maintained "The show must go on." He would conduct for the ceremony, then leave on the train next day for the funeral on Tuesday. This he did, his face all through like a mask.

"Next morning, before the train time, he came into the printing office where I worked, to bid me goodbye. He took my hand with a firm grip and held it for what seemed like a long time, looking me in the eye, and said: "Well, Dave, I've enjoyed knowing you, and we've had a lot of fun together, I want you to always think kindly of me, no matter what happens"..and he was gone, I never saw him again.

"The first intimation that all was not quite as it should be came when the florist at Spokane, from whom a wreath had been ordered by wire, wrote to say they could not locate any such funeral in the city. Then one of the men who had been an active worker with Ted remarked to another member, "You know, he borrowed $15 from me before he left. Said he was a little short, and with the funeral expenses, etc....

Hope he gets back here soon."

"Is that so," replied the other, " Well, I loaned him $25." On further inquiry it developed he had "borrowed" whatever he could from as many of the members as he was able to contact. Sums varied from $5 to as high as $50, but that chap was smart enough to demand his violin as security.

"This was the last Cranbrook ever saw of Ted Leaward, but about a year later, who should step off the train one fine day onto the station platform but the corpse—"Mama." She proceeded to take over a small restataurant on Van Horne Street—the "Waterfront," as it was often referred to then. Upstairs were several rooms which she rented out to a number of attractive younger ladies.

"Apparently she had a list of all those from whom Ted had "borrowed"money, and as her business venture progressed, she began to pay off these debts one by one. As was to be expected, the first man contacted was the one who was holding the violin. However, when asked about Ted's whereabouts she became absolutely dumb.

"How long she might have stayed in our fair city we will never know. The reason—in a few months time the town authorities suggested she move on—they were not impressed with her "roomers" upstairs. And so Madam Ted Leawards also disappeared from the Cranbrook scene, to the best of my knowledge, she never returned.

"As I was about the only one closely associated with him whom he did not attempt to proposition, I may have a little different attitude than the others, for I still hold him in high regard, and prefer to remember him for his many likeable and wonderful qualities. And were he alive today, which I doubt, I would be most happy to shake his hand again."

Ted Leaward was too good to be true. He was able to fill the role as a talented musician, band leader and teacher. Not only did he dupe his friends for money, but he led a double life. He was a con man and a connoisseur in his trade. He was not an evil man, he was just able to call the tunes and play the strings his way.

WHAT'S IN A NAME

What do horse thievery, bums and a bend in the river got to do with Ta Ta Creek, Bummers Flats and Yahk? Well, there's a story behind these names and history will reveal why they are called that today.

Place names of towns, cities and geographical locations have a history all their own. Sometimes their names are attached to the birth places and backgrounds of the prominent men who discovered the area; others are named for geographical or environmental factors, and lastly a few stem from the memory of serendipitous events.

First Nations people of any particular region had and still have, in many cases, their own names for places in their distinct dialect. Many place names have incorporated First Nation words into the English version. Many towns were initially named for places far away, like the mother country England, a place that conjured up memories, an event in time, or a word that described the physical landscape.

So often in history, stories get passed down through word of mouth. One such story about Ta Ta Creek was published by L.P. Sullivan, founder and editor of the *Cranbrook Courier*. He commissioned a reporter by the name of John Campbell to get the story about Ta Ta Creek and the following was published under a column heading "Reminiscences of Kootenay Pioneers" in the *Cranbrook Courier* of September 14, 1923. The name used in the story was fictitious to perhaps keep the person's identity a secret, but the story stands.

"Among the less frequent habitués of Fort Steele before the turn of the century was one Red Fletnum. It is not recorded of Fletnum that he was a really bad man, although there were those who suspected his tendency to err in the matter of horses. Red was simply that kind of fellow who could readily mistake another man's horses for his own. Certainly, horses were worth but little; so little, in fact, that many prospectors scarcely troubled to round them up in the spring, deeming it cheaper to purchase new stock. Therefore Fletnum eked out a precarious livelihood in picking up stray ponies and selling them for what he could get. No one minded much until, grown bold by reason of long immunity from punishment, Red sallied forth into Montana and annexed a bunch of ponies belonging to a rancher of Tobacco Plains.

The horse thief was scarcely across the boundary with his loot when the rancher became appraised of his loss. Furious with indignation, he saddled up and rode to the sheriff's office.

"A horse thief from Canada has run off my horses," he roared. He's hittin' the breeze for Fort Steele, hell for leather." The sheriff decided to take a chance. "All right, he said, let's head for Fort Steele too."

Red must have made excellent time with his stolen stock for no trace of him did his pursuers see along the trail. They learned, however, on arrival at the Canadian town, that Red Fletnum had a cabin on the west bank of the Kootenay river about fifteen miles north. (In the vicinity of what is now called the Skookumchuck Prairie).

Adding the provincial constable to their posse, the pursuers crossed the ferry over the Kootenay and were again on the trail. The constable was a great help. He knew the country and he knew Red.

Towards nightfall, on approaching Red's cabin, they sighted the horse thief himself in the very act of rounding up the stolen horses, evidently with the intention of driving them back into the mountains. Quietly they rode up to the unsuspecting outlaw.

"Hands up- you're under arrest," yelled the constable.

"Don't shoot", replied Red. "You've got the drop on me," and he slid from the horse. "I guess I know when I'm licked."

"You ain't going to take me back to Steele now, are ye" asked Red innocently.

"You'll wait till morning won't you?"

"We're going back this minute," replied the constable. "Pile on your horse and we'll travel.

"Judas Priest! said Red, "what's all the hurry? I'm tired as h—l; bin ridin' all day and I'm plumb tuckered out. At least gimme a chance to change horses; that critter I've climbed down from ain't fit to carry me five miles. It's nothing less than sinful to ride a poor brute to death.

"It was true–Red's horse was mighty tired, and the constable knew it.

"All right." said the limb of the law finally, "rope up a fresh horse and we'll travel."

"In a jiffy, the outlaw was astride a fresh horse and the little cavalcade was on its way to Fort Steele and the lockup. A short distance from Red's Camp they had to cross a small stream which ran through a heavily wooded little gully with a steep side. As they picked their way cross, Red suddenly gave vent to a loud whoop, and putting spurs to his horse, he galloped away.

"Ta ta, friends, I've business up the trail."

Red was gone–his swift mount had carried him quickly from sight among the thick-standing pines, the posse on their jaded ponies left far in the rear.

And Red's parting salute echoes in the land to this day."

The name, Ta Ta Creek, remains to this day, for a small hamlet north of Kimberley, British Columbia.

The story about Bummer's Flats stems from the early days of mining on the Wild Horse. Bummer's Flats refers to a geographical location on the East side of the Kootenay River, North West of Fort Steele. The name, according to records from the British Columbia Government Geographical Name Details, dates back to the trail days and has its own bit of quirky history.

In the mining days of the Wild Horse Creek area, there were those who made their own way and some who rode on the backs of others. According to Mrs. Clara Graham, an early pioneer and author, the story of Bummer's Flats goes like this.

"Some ne'er do wells instead of proceeding to Wild Horse simply camped in the vicinity where they "bummed" drinks, meals, etc from more affluent and generous minded travelers, or indeed anyone who would give them a dime or a drink."

With this bit of history, Bummer's Flats was so named, and is still called that today. The mining opportunities provided the backdrop for this place. The native grasses, the willows and the sloughs make up the landscape, unaffected by the lifestyle of a "bum" who attributed to this place's history. The name Bummers Flats was adopted on January 17, 1951, according to official records, and is still used today.

Yahk, a small town in Southeastern British Columbia, has no significant event in history linked to its name. It was a large logging operation incorporating flumes to float timber as well as being a point on the railway. Some sources say that the word Yahk was derived from a First Nations word, Yaak, meaning "bow" which referred to a bend in the river. In the Ktunaxa language, the word for arrow is a:k. The word Yahk may have had more than one meaning depending on the spelling. Other spellings consisted of Yak, Yaak, and Yaht.

At the turn of the century, Yahk was a thriving sawmill town caught up in the boom of the developing West. The town remains much smaller than in its heyday, but the popularity of its name today has coined a popular saying, and the phrase "I've been to Yahk and back," has became a B.C. truism.

Moyie
Some place names come down to language and environment. They stem from what people called particular environments due to conditions found at the time of exploration, or personal

experiences. The town of Moyie is a prime example. Named by a French trapper in the Thompson expedition, the word is from the French verb *mouiller* meaning to wet. The Moyie River Valley, with Moyie Lake, and the many creeks draining into it, unlike the aridity of the Rocky Mountain Trench, would have presented this association.

The BC Geographical Names gives us these details regarding Moyie Lake.

"Moyie Lakes (not Mooyie Lakes) adopted in the 2nd Report of the Geographic Board of Canada, 30 June 1900. Distinguished as Upper Moyie Lake and Lower Moyie Lake on BC map 4d,1912. Labelled Moyie Lake (singular) on BC map1EM, 1915 et seq, applying to both waterbodies. Even though these are distinct waterbodies separated by a 1-mile section of the Moyie River, the singular form "Moyie Lake" is the entrenched local name, and has appeared as such in gazetteers from 1930 onward."

It may have been originally pronounced as 'mooYay' but the one that is commonly used is 'moyEE'.

It is interesting to note that the word moil, "to labour in the mire" (circa 1400) is also possibly from the French word mouiller— to wet, moisten and the latin "molliare and "molis" meaning soft. It is easy to imagine the wet, moist conditions that confronted the early explorers—the dense cedars, willows, hawthorns, poplars, cottonwoods and all the other vegetation in the wet and lush Moyie River Valley. One of the earliest written accounts, by J. A Lees and Clutterbuck, has this to say about the Moyie valley. "Our first day was cold and wet, with great wreath of mist hanging low about the surrounding mountains and everything looking gloomy in the extreme." And regarding the Moyie trail Clutterbuck writes: " The ground was so wet that we had to put all our things, including the fire, on rafts of logs to hold them out of the water." So, it seems, from the beginning, Moyie would be linked to the word wet.

The most historic association of the name, Moyie, is with the S.S. Moyie Sternwheeler, a National Historic Site, that is one of the main tourist attractions in Kaslo, B.C. It was one of the last remaining vessels that plied Kootenay Lake.

The spelling has remained the same. The lakes remain joined by the narrows; although distinctly two bodies of water, the North and South ends, it is still referred to as Moyie Lake. The river and creeks still flow into this body of water and in one respect Moyie remains linked back to a personal experience of the landscape, named for the environment and conditions that presented themselves at the time. Wet.

CAMEL NOT

Yes, it is true, there is a link between camels and British Columbia's history. In the early 1860's, they were imported to be used as pack animals in the Cariboo area of British Columbia, as well as having been successfully used by the military in the southern states. The following tells the story of one of these beasts in the Kootenay region, and explains why the match between animal and environment was not to be. This is an excerpt from the book *Fur and Gold in the Kootenays* written by Clara Graham, an early pioneer of the Kootenay region of Southeastern British Columbia.

"Camels in the Kootenays"

"It appears that in 1868 or thereabouts four of those animals were brought from the Cariboo into East Kootenay, evidently by John Galbraith, and it has been said that when they appeared on Bummer's Flats, off the ferry boat, they created great excitement in a nearby Indian camp.

"As pack animals they were not a success for more reasons than one, principal of which appears to have been that they scared the horses and mules which they met on narrow mountain trails, also, as they were not used to the rough, mountainous country, they developed sore feet.

"Eventually three were taken to Flathead Lake, while one lost itself and wintered all alone up Cherry Creek. One tale relates that this camel grew, in the course of that winter, a very luxuriant coat of hair to protect it from the cold winds and wintry weather and one day following spring a very strange looking animal appeared upon the horizon and startled those who beheld what they thought was an apparition.

"The camel was wild and allowed no one to approach near enough to catch it. This animal, however, was too valuable to lose and besides if it were allowed to run wild the pack trains would stampede, as indeed they already had done each time they had beheld this odd-looking creature. In spite of all the schemes that had been tried in order to catch it the camel still remained free and captain of its destiny until one day a French Canadian arrived on the scene. He talked to it in his native tongue, but it will not be necessary to translate the uncomplimentary and sulphurous language this man used. Suffice it to say that the camel was delighted to meet a kindred spirit who spoke a language that it understood and, without any further ceremony, it approached the man, knelt down for him to mount and together they journeyed on to Tobacco Plain."

The eventual fate of this particular beast remains a mystery. One has to wonder whether, over time, training and acclimatization would win the camels back. Perhaps some things are not meant to be and the harsh rocky environment was the last straw that did break the camel's back and the link to British Columbia's history.

NUGGETS OF NEWS A LA 1900

Newspapers were the bulletin boards of the day. From advertising to proclaiming news of what was new, from who came or went to town to opportunities that lay ahead for enterprising entrepreneurs, it was the life line and often the only line in town. We get a picture of the small happenings, the to and fro of a developing city in its cradle days. Somewhat like a town crier, these nuggets of news portray Nelson, British Columbia, in its infancy, boasting its successes and crying out for continued development.
From *The Miner*–June 21, 1890.

"Small Nuggets of News"

"G. O Buchanan has received a new carriage for his saw–mill, and now cuts lumber as smooth as a politician's promises.

Dan O'Ray has two contracts on his hands. One is supplying the Galena with wood: the other, the mosquitoes with blood.

Somehow some people who have more notoriety than reputation hanker after conspicuous locations for their shanties. Suppose they be compelled to take a back seat behind the rocky bluffs.

Bonner's Ferry is the place where the boys go out to have a little social game of "stud" or "draw". Some of them come back wishing they hadn't made the trip.

Railway contractors may have soft snaps once and awhile; but that old-time contractor who was herding a gang of Chinese shovelers on a one–by–one–slope back of Sproat the other day, with the sun 105 in the shade, hadn't that kind of snap. We'll gamble that he wished he was back in Manitoba raising Jersey Ayrshire bulls.

A.D. Wheeler of Ainsworth, a man who has done much to help develop and attract attention to the Hot Springs mining district since his arrival there in 1884, was married to Miss Sutton at Tacoma, Washington, on the 11th. The bride is a sister to Mrs. G.B.Wright. Mr. and Mrs. Wheeler arrived home on the Galena Thursday, and were welcomed by a salute of 20 giant powder guns.

A.J. Marks returned Thursday, via Revelstoke and Sproat, from a month's trip to the coast. He reports purchasing furniture for a 40-foot addition to the Nelson house, of which he and Mr. Van Ness are owners.

Hume and Co. are having their building plastered. The lime was brought in from Spokane and the sand from near "Bogustown". C.J. Branch of Revelstoke is doing the work. It might be worth the while of some man to prospect around here for lime-rock and a site for a kiln.

A watchmaker and jeweler might make a living in one of the towns in this district, provided he did not want the earth all at once.

Of all Nelson's many palatial business houses but 3 are adorned with signs—Harris's shoe shop, the Kootenay hotel, and the Nelson house. This is a pointer for some enterprising sign painter.

Thursday Joe Wilson's pack train cleaned up all Nelson freight at Sproat and brought it up the north side of the river, crossing it at the falls instead of at Ward's ferry.

George Bigelow is out at Spokane Falls and Victoria purchasing goods for his Nelson store. He will probably take in Olympia, Washington, on the trip, as that is said to be a good place in which to buy umbrellas and type writers.

Two of the 3 owners of The Miner owe their lives to Henry Blair. Late one night last March when footsore and weary from trudging over the rocks and boulders that line the north bank of the Kootenay river between Bob Yuill's camp and the point opposite Nelson, they were met by Mr. Blair and rescued. It was a timely rescue for one of the two has been "tired" ever since.

R. E. Lemmon is in Victoria purchasing stock for his Nelson house. The goods will be shipped in via Kootenai station and Bonner's Ferry.

The shares in the Citizen's wharf at Nelson would be above par if the same rate of wharfage was charged for landing goods on it as is charged by the Canadian Pacific for landings made at the wharf at Sproat.

C.S.F. Hamber came in Thursday from New Westminster, and will engage in the real estate business. He was accompanied by a fishing rod only.

" Captain" Davies intends docking the Midge for repairs. The machinery will be sent out to Portland, Oregon, for a thorough overhauling. The hull will be recaulked and repainted. These improvements will make the Midge the smartest craft of her size in inland British Columbia.

Jim Gilker, Nelson's genial postmaster, requests The Miner to publish broadcast that her majesty's mail arrives at his office every Monday at 4 o'clock and departs every Tuesday morning at 7:30 o'clock. Letters for registry should be handed in at least 30 minutes before the time for departure.

Nelson undoubtedly can boast of a larger number of buildings than any other town in the district, but it cannot hold a candle to Ainsworth for boats. At the latter place can be found sail boats, punts, row boats, canoes of canvass and of bark, bateaux, etc, etc. finished in all styles and painted in all colors.

An engine and flat car for the Sproat to Nelson railway was brought down by the Kootenai on Thursday.

Ed Atherton is seriously thinking of writing a novel. It will be founded on his narrow escape from drowning the last time the Slocan ferry went out, and will be entitled, "Saved–Without Wetting a Hair."

E.E. Alexander of Spokane Falls is in Nelson looking after his mining interests. He also intends purchasing lots at the auction sale on the 25th."

All these nuggets of development and entrepreneurial beginnings in the 1900s laid the foundation for the city it is today, Nelson, the Queen City of the Kootenays.

OF CATS AND GRIZZLIES

Stories about animals of the wild are always revealing. Here are two stories that express an unusual view. Wild animals have always put the fear in man and rightly so. They have their world and we have ours. The truth is, we have more to fear from accidental mishaps of the human variety than encounters with the "big bad wolf."

These stories both appeared in the *Crag and Canyon* of August, 1903. They were written by Chauncey Thomas, a writer of wildlife stories. This story first appeared in the *Saturday Evening Post*.

"A Mountain Lion's Courage"

"As for the Mountain Lion, there is not a greater coward in the west, not excepting the valiant coyote. A twenty pound dog can run any Mountain lion up a tree; and he will become nothing but a yellow streak of retreat before an ordinary ram, even though hungry and with a fat lamb to be had for the taking. He is dangerous only to colts, calves and dead horses.

"One or two of these man eaters used to meow about our cabin, but not one of the half dozen of the experienced miners there paid any attention to them, nor was there a gun in the camp. None of us had any fear of going down the gulch through the timber for the mails and supplies, usually alone and after dark. Their yowls— which sound like those of a tom cat in a barrel—give you the creeps—but what of that? So does the filing of a saw. In winter we might have carried a gun after dark, but not if we had a load to bring back. Under circumstances I have known that same enlarged backyard cry to cause a party of tenderfeet–thoroughly informed as to their danger—to sit up all night between two huge fires, clothed in firearms and gooseflesh. The account of their narrow escape no doubt made thrilling reading matter, one page of which, blowing languidly down the gulch, would have made the cause of it adjourn to the next township.

"I never heard of anyone being hurt by a Mountain lion. In fact, the only case I know of where any of the cat tribe attacked a man was on the headwaters of the Troublesome in the summer of 1891. A wild cat—the common twenty-pound bob-tail suddenly leaped from a tree down on to the shoulders of a range rider. It scratched him up a little and he killed it with a club. That such a thing was very unusual may be judged from the fact that the incident was told of for a hundred miles in every direction, and was accounted for only on the assumption that the cat was mad; that is a case of animal insanity.

"Danger is like a rumor or a river; the closer you get to its source the smaller it becomes. It is the same with the bear and the Mountain lion. In roaming over the wildest regions of the Rockies there is but one real danger: that of getting hurt and no one finding you till too late, perhaps never. A sprained ankle, a broken leg, puts the lone hunter in more danger than all the bears and Mountain lions whose bad reputations—on paper—ever made the tenderfoot's teeth chatter or turned his scalp into a pinecushion."

"Fighting Qualities of the Grizzly"

"Perhaps my idea of the modern grizzly—who makes no attempt to live up to the reputation established by his more foolish ancestors—is because, try as I might, I never managed to get into but one bear mix- up, and that was a very mild affair, too tame to tell of. In the beginning I was bashful about intruding on his awful presence, but I soon found that he was the more deferent of the two; in fact that he always retired at the rate of thirty miles and hour. I was the more careful because I had heard that he, when wounded, and often when not, would charge a man, especially if the man lolled young and tender. Well, this is so, except that the bear, due, no doubt, to his long contact with advancing civilization—at the end of a gun barrel of course—like all other primitive races has at last adopted modern methods of warfare and has given up the frontal attack. He tries to attack you from the rear by going around the earth; and as he has some distance to go he loses no time about it.

"Coolness, caution and caliber—these are the three essentials in a bear scrap, and the heavier the caliber, the better, for when old Ephraim does wake up only a brain or a backbone shot will stop that foaming charge. You may riddle that desperate heart to pulp—a lathered yellow chop-chop, a tree splitting blur of paws, and where the hunter stood only a reeking something quivers. If you run from a lightning bear you are a dead man; if he turns on you it is either man or bear. One must die instantly. But all this was in the long ago and in the modern newspaper. Nowadays when a bear feels bored he promptly migrates. His ruling passion is horizon hunger, and between his tribe and mankind he has drawn the sky line."

THE MOUNTAIN-CLIMBING GIRL

Women who loved the mountains, who loved to climb, and had just as much adventurous spirit as the men, were usually not given much mention in the history books. There were a few exceptions, like Mary Schäffer Warren, who, convention aside, allowed her love of the West and adventurous spirit of exploration to discover the jewels of mountain life. These women didn't follow the rules and prescription of the times, but followed their own hearts and love of nature.

While the names of early guides in the Rocky Mountains are well known to some, the women who were at the dawn of the developing West, and climbed peaks with the best, were hardly recognized for their astonishing zeal for the mountains.

The following poem published in a very early *Crag and Canyon* pays a bit of a tribute to those very eccentric women.
"The Mountain–Climbing Girl"

> "We read about the seashore girl down
> where the breakers play
> Who listens to proposals six or seven
> times a day;
> The summer girl who flits about the
> "Boarders Taken" farms,
> The cycle girl with sawed -off skirts
> exhibiting her charms.
> The picnic girl is bold and sweet, the
> mother girl is wise,
> The golf girl wins admirers with her
> strokes--and with her eyes,
> But in the ranks of girly girls there is

no fairer pearl
In all the whole kaboodle than the
mountain- climbing girl.

Her face is delicately brown from kisses
From the sun,
Her eyes are ever twinkling with the
Merry light of fun,
Her laugh is like the babbling brooks in
which she loves to wade,
Her shoes and stockings on the bank in
neat confusion laid.
Her song is sweet as notes of birds that
watch her from the trees,
It rings as liquid music on the ever-
bracing breeze;
She's brave as any lion and as nimble as
a squir'l
That Western bunch of energy, the
mountain-climbing girl.

At break of day she'll hit the trail
with alpenstock in hand,
Her face a charming picture by the
early breezes fanned,
and up the rugged steeps she'll climb
with never-tiring powers,
Oft lying with an open book upon a bed
of flowers.
Through wildest gorge, in canyon dark
and up the rocky steep,
Along the creek whose waters bright
o'er boulders dash and leap.
And where the brooks from hidden
springs go down with silent swirl

She goes upon her daily jaunts, the
mountain-climbing girl.
Anon she'll pause to pluck a burr that's
clinging to her hose,
Or pluck from off its parent stem a
fragrant mountain rose.
And when that lazy feeling comes lie
down for cat-nap sleep,
Nor fear in that wild, lovely spot that
eyes are near to peep.
She'll roam till gathering shadows
herald the approach of night,
Then hasten home to supper with a
hired man's appetite.
The smoking pork and beans she'll hit a
gastronomic whirl--
Oh! She's a hefty feeder, is the
mountain-climbing girl!

The haughty belle of fashion in her
tailor-fitted gown
May ridicule this jewel with the hands
and face so brown.
May laugh in queenly manner at her
rough, loose-fitting clothes,
And sneer to see the redness of her
little sun-peeled nose.
But let them laugh as freely as their
corsets will allow,
They cannot snatch a laurel of wild
beauty from her brow;
The ones who think her horrid aren't
really fit to curl
The breeze-entangled frizzes of the
mountain-climbing girl."

Mary Schäffer with horse, Whyte Museum of the Canadian Rockies (V527/PS-151)

MEMORIES, RESOLUTIONS &
CHRISTMASES OF YORE

Memories of times past, resolutions, and hopes for the future are as relevant to our world today as they were to those living a century ago.

Sarah Larue Galbraith was the wife of John Galbraith, one of the earliest pioneers to the Fort Steele area of southeastern British Columbia. It was John Galbraith who built the first building for the Hudson's Bay Company at what was then called Galbraith's Ferry and later called Fort Steele, British Columbia. It was to this log cabin that John Galbraith took his bride. She arrived from Walla Walla, having travelled over 400 miles on horseback. Perhaps this feat alone shows her rugged determination and spirit, not to mention her strong will and stamina. She was one of the first white women settlers in the area.

In a short story she sent to the *Cranbrook Courier*, she recalled her fond memories of the Christmas she spent at Galbraith's Ferry in 1869. It is a telling historical perspective from one of the early pioneering women. Here are her words.

"It is near Christmas. I am thinking of the first Christmas I spent on the banks of the Kootenay River at John Galbraith Ferry, now Fort Steele. The river was almost frozen over. One could walk on the ice with almost perfect safety. It was bitter cold with the thermometer at between 30 and 40 below zero.

"Despite the rigors of winter, it was great fun to watch the old Indian women fishing through the ice. Fishing was good. Every so often would come out of the river a good sized trout. This process was repeated several times showing the river was well stocked with trout.

"In the early days of the ferry, we had always plenty of wild game on the porch, trout deer, wild goat, wild mountain sheep, bear meat, and buffalo meat. Our table was plentifully supplied with game birds, Mallard ducks, and wild geese aplenty. The first wild gray goose I had ever eaten was cooked in front of an open fire. We did not enjoy the privileges we have nowadays. We had no cook stoves then. We cooked in the frying pan, baked bread in front of the big, hot coals. Then my husband would bake his favourite bread in the gold pans. It was the best bread I ever ate. I like that kind of life. The miners would come by the ferry and camp all night, on their way to Walla, Walla, with their cantinas (saddle bags) full of gold dust, or two or three buckskin pouches full of rich dust or nuggets. I was the only white woman there in 1869, as the few women who came in, left for the winter, some never to return.

"The grey goose was the best roasted goose I ever had for a Christmas dinner, with plum pudding and Martell's brandy sauce from Sam Hardley's Hudson Bay store, just a mile above the ferry. There was only three of us for dinner, Mr. Fossit, Mr. Galbraith and myself, as most of the men had gone away for the winter. We didn't have any of the good Irish potatoes or cabbage or other vegetables that they grow in the Kootenays nowadays. The regular ration was made up of just bread, bacon, and beans and plenty of wild game.

"Permit me to extend to the old-timers and the recent arrivals the Compliments of The Season, and to wish them well in the Kootenay."

Mrs. S.L.Galbraith.

The *Cranbrook Courier* published this story entitled, "Christmas Bells In the Little Log Cabin by the River", on Dec 23, 1929.

The following is a love poem that was sent to the *Cranbrook Herald* by one of its readers. Love poems and nostalgia seem to transcend the years.

"Fifty Years Ago"
"It seems but yesterday, dear one,
You made your promise true.
We had a wedding at the church,
And asked the friends we knew.
But few are left to celebrate,
And few are left to go,
Who wished us joy and happiness
Just fifty years ago.

"We planned our quiet little world
 Around our country home.
There were no modern gadgets then
No gas or telephone.
The woodbox stood beside the door.
Its contents seldom low;
The lamps were trimmed and filled by you
Just fifty years ago.

"The papers came but once a week,
There were no radios;
We never heard of nightclubs then
Or even picture shows.
I saddled up the old grey mare,
And rode a mile or so
To get supplies and fetch the mail
Some fifty years ago.

"We had our share of blessedness;
We had our share of pain;
And many of our joys we knew
Cannot come back again.
But memories fill my life, my dear,
Each day they dearer grow
The things we did, just you and I
Just fifty years ago.

"We two have traveled down the years,
We're growing older now,
And time and care have left their mark
On hand and heart and brow.
But you are just as fair to me,
I love you more I know,
Than when you promised you'd be mine
Just fifty years ago."

New Year's Resolutions

These words were written on the brink of a new century. Their sentiment and goodwill are still prevalent today.

"Resolve not to be critical.

Resolve to be liberal-minded.

Resolve that the world is full of people as good as yourself, and that you are as good as any of them.

Resolve to give other people credit for their opinions, even if they do differ from you.

Resolve to say a kind word when the opportunity offers.

Resolve to quit lying, unless you can do yourself or someone else good by it.

Resolve that the member of any other church probably stands as well as you do in the eyes of the Lord.

Resolve if you are a single man, to get married as soon as you can find a good woman foolish enough to have you.

Resolve if you are a single woman, to cultivate those traits that will make you a good wife instead of a gossiping busybody.

Resolve, if you are a married woman, to say a few kind words about your acquaintances, instead of roasting them at every opportunity.

Resolve, if you are a preacher, that you have not a monopoly on the transportation to heaven, and that there may be others who say less and do more.

Resolve to be decent and manly, even if you have to give up some of your bad habits.

Resolve to be on the square. It won't hurt you.

Resolve to show more humanity and less cussedness in your make-up.

Resolve (and remember this one) to take your paper home."

From the *Cranbrook Herald,* Dec, 1900

FISHING TALES & POETRY

No matter what the century, fishing stories are a genre all their own. The storyteller gets us hooked with the action, the strike, the fight and the size. Casting and luring us in for the catch. A good one, we hope. These words have let their lines out long ago and reeled their catch in, or sometimes not, but they too have their own tale to spin and lines that reel the centuries together.

Crag and Canyon, May 7, 1904
"Fisherman's Monologue"

"Row slowly now—A little nearer to the shore—There, that's right—Steady, now.

This eddy looks like a good place—The left oar, just a little—There, that's fine. Just by these lilypads a large one was caught the other day, Gee Whiz! Did you see that? A strike, and he was a beauty too. An eight pounder, I'll bet. Back water, quick, till I try him again. Steady, now this is the place—I guess, we've missed him. No, by jove! There he was again. He's got it! He's got it! Turn her out into deep water. He's in the lilypads now, and a goner, sure. Thunderation! And, man, he was such a monster. Must have weighed at least ten pounds. No, there he is. He is still hooked. He is all right. He is free from the lilies—he is free. Steady now, put the oars in the boat. See the pole, he bends it nearly double. And doesn't he make the reel sing. Now he has turned. He is making towards us. Hand me that landing net. Quick! Quick! He is going under the boat. He will snap the line. Holy Smoke! There he goes. Grab the line. Grab the line, I say. Have you got it? Keep him fast now. Just a second. Steady, now. There he goes into the net. Here he is in the boat. We have him, he is safe. And isn't he a beauty, a peach. He will go above six pounds if he goes an ounce. Wasn't he lively? Did you see him make that three foot leap out of the water? You didn't? Man, where were your eyes? Row in now, and we will take him up to the Sanitarium and weigh him. How much did you say? Four pounds and two ounces—Pshaw! That can't be right. Your scales are not accurate. Well, he's a beauty anyway. It took a full half-hour to tire him out and land him. Three minutes, you say. Oh! You're mistaken, that can't possibly be. He was surely longer than that. Naw; not a bit. Cool as a cucumber, just as I am now. He certainly is a beauty though."

Crag and Canyon, May 14, 1904

"A Fishing Story"

"I'll spin you a yarn. Yes, sir, it's the truth. Last summer I was rubbering down the Bow, one day when all the sports were out, and the man I got on the end of a line was the biggest in the river. You just ought to have seen him. I've had plenty of luck, but, this old fellow beat the record. I found him a little way up the river, not far from the creek, he was lurking there. My! But he was a gamey rascal. I bet he weighed 300 pounds if he weighed an ounce.

"I got a clear look at him when I started to play him and he was fully seven feet, with a beautiful red and purple color around the gills. And gamey? Say, he was something fierce!

"As soon as I felt him strike I knew I had a tough proposition. For a time I thought he was going to have me in the air. But I held on and commenced to play with him in my best style. I knew I had him secure so he couldn't let go, and the only question was whether I could tire him out.

"You can judge of his size when I tell you he hauled me clear round his boat twice, and I had to hold on tight or he would have got clean away.

"Just as I began to feel that he was getting tired and I was beginning to think how fine he'd look in a photograph hanging up beside me, the line parted and I had to let him go. It was a shame, wasn't it? I'll never rely on those dinky little silk lines again. There'll be sport if ever I get him on the end of a line again. If any of you fellows think you've had fun with a fresh young guy, or one of those five-foot city dudes, wait till you see the man I nearly caught. I had him good and proper. And I'd have him up home now preserved in a frame and neatly varnished ---If the bloomin' line hadn't broke."

Arlene Pervin

Crag and Canyon June 4, 1904

"A Born Fisherman"

"Too tired to work,
Too tired to walk;
Too tired to read,
Too tired to talk,
Too tired to eat,
Too tired to drink,
Too tired to write,
Too tired to think.
Too tired to ride,
Too tired to row,
Too tired to stay,
Too tired to go,
To tired to want,
Too tired to wish,
But never too tired
To-sit-an'-fish."

Crag and Canyon June 4, 1904
" A Pleasant Fishing Party"

"A very happy trio of fishermen in the shape of three ambassadors of commerce from Winnipeg pulled off from W. Mather's boat house last Monday morning. The party consisted of Messrs. E. M. Christie, Geo. Wilson, and A.E. Carmichael. Following the stream up into a narrow entrance of Vermillion lake, here the three sportsmen threw in their lines for unsuspecting trout. The game went merrily on until Mr. Carmichael suddenly got a nibble as the float on his line told. The nibble turned into a good strong tug which told in silent words the rest of the party that the lucky fisherman had Mr. Trout hooked. Now, Mr. Carmichael never told the rest of the party that this trip was his debut in the finny circles, though intimately acquainted with fishing tackle of all descriptions. On Mr. Carmichael getting the fish well hooked, he let a yell out of him that would have done credit to a red man of 1885, and with a tremendous pull the trout was landed, not on the bank or in the boat, but into the lap of a lady belonging to another party who were fishing beside him.

"The lady proved herself a fisherman, for quietly unhooking the trout she dropped him into her own basket with a thank you. The above little event was soon forgot when Mr. Wilson was seen in a hot fight with a monster on the end of his line, for he proved such after a 20 minute fight tipping the scales at 3 ½ pounds. The catch of the day ran to 40 odd, many going to 2 to 2 ½ pounds."

OF MEN AND INK

They say that men are called to religion or the priesthood, but one can say the same for early newspaper men, men who were driven to write. Their wit, humour and flair for opinion drove them to print. So, they set up newspapers wherever they put down roots.

It is a story of guts, determination, men and ink. Newspaper men put their lives on the line. From the threat of losing their subscribers because of something they wrote, to papers going bust; from libel cases that ran through the courts, to plain being run out of town. These ups and downs rarely deterred their stamina as men or their love affair with the printed word.

Whether it was the lure of the gold pans, the Rocky Mountains or the frontier of the Wild West, the men who set up shop to print the local newspapers were also inevitably entrepreneurs, editors, and ambassadorial promoters of the small towns in which they lived. These men were usually eccentric characters, opinionated, with a savoir faire about publishing a newspaper. The skillful craft of being able to tell a good story was key to their game.

The following is a story about four legendary newspaper men:Fred Smyth, Robert Lowery, Bob Edwards and Norman Luxton. All these men have one trait in common. In the words of Mark Twain it is called temperament and circumstance. Each of their stories will reveal a combination of both these elements. All these newspaper men were drawn to the West, set up newspapers in small fledgling towns and wrote about the times and issues of the day by exposing their views on political, moral and social fronts. The following are their words and stories.

Arlene Pervin

FRED SMYTH—Of DRIVE & DETERMINISM

F. J. Smyth *Cranbrook Herald*, April 19th, 1906

Frederick J. Smyth was born on October 1, 1872 in Huntington, Quebec. His family moved to Walla Walla, Washington, where they ranched on the Snake River. At nineteen, Fred made his way to Pullman, Washington where he got a job in a printing office. This was the start of his lifelong connection to newspaper work. Along the way, he worked for Sandon, Nelson, Kaslo, Phoenix, Hazelton, Queen Charlottes Islands, Princeton, Sandpoint and Grand Forks newspapers. He was best known as founder and editor of the *Moyie Leader* which ran from 1898 to 1911. His drive and determination in coming to Moyie and setting up shop is best told in his own words. The following is excerpted from his own book, *Tales of the Kootenays*.

"My coming to Moyie and East Kootenay early in 1898 was brought about in this way: The legislature at Victoria had been dissolved. The Turner government was going back to the country, and an election was pending. In the Turner cabinet was Colonel James Baker, provincial secretary and minister of Education. East Kootenay was his constituency and William Baillie, a newspaper man working for A.B. Grace of the Fort Steele Prospector, received the nomination to run against Baker.

"Moyie was an important point, and Baker felt he needed all the newspaper support he could muster. He made arrangements to have a newspaper plant brought in, and I was selected to have charge of moving a plant here from Slocan City and running it after it was set up. But first I made a trip in to look over the situation and line up some business.

"Construction was pretty well along the eastern end of the Crow's Nest Pass railway, but the western end was being carried on in a section by the contractors, with open spaces between with just the right away cleared. A tote road had been built along the right of way to enable supplies being distributed to the different camps.

"I made the trip from Nelson to Kuskanook on the steamer Nelson and then walked the sixty miles to Moyie, stopping at construction camps along the way. I was a young fellow and enjoyed walking. The exercise gave me a ravenous appetite and the rough camp grub was devoured with relish. Getting a place to sleep was the greatest difficulty. One night I stopped at a camp near Kitchener. It looked as though I would have to sit up in a chair. Then the cook had a brain wave. He shoved the tin and porcelain dishes and knives and forks to one end of the long table and rustled me a blanket from somewhere. Climbing up on the table and using my coat for a pillow, I spent a fairly comfortable night. There was a big camp stove in the cook house and from time to time the night watchman would come in and stoke up with four foot lengths of Tamarac. Next morning I slipped the cook $1 for his friendly gesture.

"Completing arrangements at Moyie for starting a newspaper, I again walked back to Kuskanook to get the plant. At Kuskanook I arranged for having the newspaper plant hauled to Moyie over the tote road. E.R. Vipond provided the outfit, the front bob of a sleigh, with two long poles attached and a four horse team.

The poles dragged along in the sleigh ruts. The roads were just breaking up, so that they were neither good for sleighing or wheeling. The Army press, cases of type and other printing equipment were loaded on this improvised contraption, and away we went. I walked behind to watch for anything falling off, and thus made my third trip of walking from Kuskanook to Moyie. We were six days on the road, and when we landed at Moyie I handed Harris an even $100 for the job, and he earned every cent of it.

"My first newspaper office in Moyie was in what had been the barroom of the first hotel in the town, and run by Glen Campbell and A.T. Clark. They had just moved into their new building close by. As was then the custom, the new hotel opened with a big dance. There was no lacking of men, but a most decided dearth of ladies, for there were only seven present and in order to form two sets for a quadrille, a gentleman would have to take his turn playing the part of a lady, with a handkerchief tied around his arm. A fiddler and a fellow thumping out chords on a wheezy organ supplied the music.

"The next room to the printing office was what had been the dining room of the old hotel, and the basement was used as a jail. Drunks would be thrown in there to sober up. Later in the spring and summer when the weather was fine prisoners were taken out and chained to stumps. Two mounted police, SGT. Clopp and Constable Frank Angers, kept good order during the railway construction days.

"Moyie had wonderfully bright future prospects when I landed there in March 1898. Enough work done on the St. Eugene to give assurance that it was a real mine. Several thousand tons of ore had been taken out and piled on the dumps awaiting the completion of the railway so that it could be shipped. Most of the buildings in town were built of logs. McMahon brothers, Pat, Frank, and John, had the largest store and also ran a hotel. Campbell and Clark, Victor Desaulniers and Chas, Kauffman were running hotels. There was yet no post office and mail was left at whichever hotel was most convenient.

"One of the first delegated over the Crows Nest Branch after its completion was a party of newspaper men from the east. They travelled on a special train which stopped for a few minutes just opposite my printing office, and the newspaper sign naturally attracted the attention of the visiting journalist. One of them strolled over to have a look. It was press day and I was busy grinding out the 'weekly effort', page at a time, on a little Army press. This man, accustomed to high speed city plants, gazed a moment, then strode to the door and beckoned to his friends. 'Hey fellows! He shouted. 'Come over there and see a man turning out a newspaper on a washing machine'."

Fred Smyth published the *Moyie Leader* for 13 years. The first edition was published on 16 April, 1898 and the last ran on 28 April, 1911. After the closing of the St. Eugene mine, Fred plied his trade in various other places around British Columbia and Idaho. He returned to the Kootenays and joined the staff of the

Cranbrook Courier in 1928 where he worked for over 20 years. His popular column was called "Observations". His book, "Tales of the Kootenay," an account of early days in the area, was published in 1938 on the 40th anniversary of the coming of the railroad into Cranbrook.

It took a certain drive and optimism to start up a paper at the turn of the century. Fred Smyth was a man who showed drive and determination to follow his path. In his own words, he lays his craft on the line with a printed picture of what it took to be one of these old time editors.

"Publishing a newspaper is a fascinating game. Once you get into it its tentacles hold you in its embrace like the insatiable craving of a dope addict. You like to write and you like to see your stuff in print. There is just that much ego in your makeup, and you can't get away from it. On the subject of writing, let me quote from that excellent book, "*The Man With The Green Shade*," by Stanley Walker, eminent New York editor: 'News is as hard to hold as quicksilver, and it fades more rapidly than any morning glory. But for all that it is the best yardstick we have to hold up against the growth and decay of human lives and ideas. It is a sounding board on which love-calls and the prayers, the wishes of meanness and the trumpets of glory receive their test.

'You can train a man to write correct English. Universities do this. But you cannot train him to tell an interesting story, this gift must come naturally to him'."

A town with a newspaper gave the town a lifeline. In the early days, printing a newspaper was a laborious job, with cases of font, tins of ink and tempermental presses. Fred J. Smyth dedicated his life to his craft.

Fred Smyth was known for his tales. The following story reveals his talent as a good storyteller. "A Remarkable Fishing Trip" was published in 1915 in the *Princeton Star*, which he ran for five years for his friend Colonel R. T. Lowery.

"Twenty years ago, before the Crow's Nest Railway was built, Jim Cronin was at Moyie Lake developing the St. Eugene mine, which afterward made him a millionaire. That was before Cranbrook was on the map, and supplies had to be packed from Fort Steele. Fresh meat was scarce and Mr. Cronin depended largely on the fish caught in the lake. There are times when fish will scamper round in the water and play tag with each other, but will not grab a hook. Cronin was fishing on one of these days and became desperate. He would have some fish anyhow. A fuse cap was attached to a stick of dynamite, a match touched to the fuse and the lot thrown in the water several yards from shore.

"Now it happened that Cronin had a dog for a companion and this particular dog dearly loved to swim and bring back sticks that his master would throw in the lake. When the dog saw the stick of dynamite thrown, he did the natural thing and plunged in after it. The dog got the dynamite all right, and with the fuse still burning nicely, started for the shore to deliver it to his master. Cronin struck for the hills and kicked several jackrabbits out of his way as he ran. Mr. Cronin is still living history but history does not relate as to what became of the dog."

"When Smyth was asked whether the story was true, he replied as any master storyteller would, with "why ruin a good story?""

The following tribute to a country editor seems fitting for Frederick J. Smyth. This poem was his last "Observations", a regular column of his, printed in the *Cranbrook Courier* on July 14, 1949.

"The Country Editor" (by Robert J. Burdette)
"Oh come," I said to the printer man
Who edits the weekly Swish
"A rest will do you a lot
Of good-
So come to the creek
And fish."

"If you'll wait a while,"
Said the printer man
I'll toddle along, I think;
But first I must write up
Some local dope,
And open a can of ink.

And carry in coal for the
Stove,
And mix up a lot of paste
And clean the grease from
The printing press,
With a bushel of cotton
Waste.

And call on the doctor and
Have him soak
The swelling from my head,
For I had it punched an
Hour ago
For something the paper
Said."

"I fear," I said to the prin
terman
"If I wait till this chore
List fails
The minnows that frolic a-
Long the creek
Will be as large as whales."

Fred Smyth died on August 16, 1949. He was 76. He left a legacy
of history in print.

ROBERT THORNTON LOWERY—THE COLONEL

Pioneering newspaper man "Colonel" Robert T. Lowery (Sandon Paystreak Vol XIII Number 1)

Another pioneer man of words was R.T. Lowery, better known as the 'Colonel.' Robert Thornton Lowery was born in Halton County, Ontario, in 1859. As to the character of the man, the following excerpt published in the *Cranbrook Courier* titled "*Whiskey and Whiskers*", a book written by Wayne McCrory, attests to that.

"Old timers in the Kootenays still talk about Colonel Lowery. If you ask about the Colonel they will tell you good things and they will tell you bad things. They will tell you that he stood 60 inches from head to toe but that his strength of character made up for his small size. They will tell you that he was as wiry as a weasel and that he strutted down the main street of New Denver like a bantam rooster. They will tell you that he had a passion for booze that he played a good hand of poker and blackjack. They will tell you that "Colonel" was an honorary title because he dressed well, cultivated a goatee, and smoked two-bit cigars. Local history books will add that he was a queer genius with a caustic wit, that he was rather mild with a kindly smile, and that he had the bearing of a country parson.

"If you look at an old picture of him and study it closely you will be caught by the Irish eyes that shine behind his steel rimmed spectacles, eyes that seem to bore right through you. However, it does not matter too much about his looks and mannerisms. What is important is that he was the founder of eight Kootenay newspapers, a small monthly periodical, and a small yearly magazine. What is important too is that he wrote humorous accounts of the lives and times of early mining camps and they're like reading from Mark Twain."

Lowery settled in the Kootenays and his first B.C. newspaper was the *Kaslo Claim* printed May 12, 1893. Times were tough and the life of the *Kaslo Claim* was very short. Lowery printed its "tombstone edition" on August 25, 1893. Lowery printed the obit for his own paper and the front page had the following inscription. "Keep off the Grass. Sacred memory of the Kaslo Claim. Born on May 12, 1893. Died August 25, 1893."

Exhibiting his sense of humour in the last edition of the *Kaslo Claim*, Lowery had a bit of fun with his delinquent accounts. Those that hadn't paid, found their ads printed upside down; those who had partly paid found theirs sideways, and of course those that fully paid were printed correctly, right side up.

Not a man to stay down for long, Lowery moved his printing press to Nakusp with the first edition of the *Nakusp Ledge* rolling off the press on October 5, 1893. He hit paydirt with the *Ledge*, moving the paper to New Denver in 1894 and later to Nelson in August of 1904 and eventually to Greenwood in October of 1904.

With the boom of the 'Silvery Slocan,' the mining town of Sandon was where the action was and September 26, 1896 saw the launch of the first edition of the *Sandon Paystreak*.

Lowery had a tongue-in -cheek, sassy style and an ad promoting his *New Denver Ledge* read like this. "The Ledge is two dollars a year in advance. When not paid it is $2.50 to parties worthy of credit. Legal advertising 10 cents a nonpareil line first insertion, and 5 cents a line each subsequent insertion. Reading notices 25 cents a line, and commercial advertising graded in prices according to circumstances.

Fellow Pilgrims: The Ledge is located at New Denver, BC and can be traced to many parts of the earth. It comes to the front every Thursday has never been raided by the sheriff, snowslided by cheap silver, or submitted by the fear of man. It works for the trail blazer as well as the bay-windowed champagne flavored capitalist. It aims to be on the right side of everything and believes that hell should be administered to the wicked in large doses. It has stood the test of time, and an ever-increasing paystreak is proof that it is better to tell the truth, even if the heavens do occasionally hit our smokestack. A chute of job work is worked occasionally for the benefit of humanity and the financier. Come in and see us, but do not pat the bulldog on the cranium, chase the black crow from our water barrel; one is savage and the other victim of thirst. One of the noblest works of creation is the man who always pays the printer; he is sure of a bunk in paradise, with thornless roses for a pillow by night and nothing but gold to look at by day."

It was in this paper that Lowery voiced his sometimes controversial opinions.

In this editorial, Lowery stands up for improved conditions on behalf of the miners of the day.

"The miner is the backbone of every mining camp. It is upon the money that he earns that we, who live in the towns hard by, get our daily bread and other luxuries. It is for him principally that the saloons are fitted up in gorgeous style. It is for him that the storekeeper is waiting so that he may pay his bills. It is through his hard work that many men of capital are enabled to ride in carriages and dine with dukes in Europe. He gets $3.50 a day in the Slocan, and for this amount he pounds a drill and lacerates rocks in the darkness of the tunnel or shaft. He occasionally is assisted up the Golden Stairs by a premature blast, and sometimes gets introduced to St. Peter by the aid of a snowslide. Being of so much value to the community, his life should be freed from danger as much as possible. One way to do this is to have all the buildings at the mines built in such a manner as to obviate the danger from slides, and render it unnecessary for men to flee for their lives, as has been done during the past week.

"Miners may be plentiful, and some capitalists may think that their lives cut but a small figure, but we think different. We want every one of them to have a chance to die in bed, and we urge upon all owners the necessity of seeing that their employees are protected from the danger of slides in every possible way. Take our advice, boys, or when the slides come again, some of you may have to push clouds instead of holding the end of a drill."

Sandon was known as the "Monte Carlo" of Canada for its gambling and Lower Sandon housed one of the largest red light districts in the region. The 'Colonel' did not shy away from the reality of the day. His opinion on legalizing prostitution is evident from this editorial of 1897.

"It would seem more sensible and honest to face the problem of prostitution and if it cannot be suppressed and prohibited, then regulate it. Prostitution is no more a normal moral condition of womankind than leprosy or cancer are normal conditions of the human race. Go into the sweatshops and awful dens in the large cities where women, girls and children sew garments together for 12 and 14 hours daily at a wage from 20 to 40 cents a day. Read the statistics furnished by the Commissioner of Labour each year, which tells of the miseries of the two-dollar-a-week factory operatives, of the tenement house life within whose noisome purlieu moral death stalks as a pestilence, and you will not wonder that there are so many poor prostitutes, but rather that there are so few.

"It is more humane, more honourable for the municipality to take cognizance of the prostitute as an inseparable part of this barbarism we call civilization and deal with her from the standpoint, than to make the stupid pretence that she has no existence simply because the law recognizes her only as a criminal."

Lowery's sarcastic wit, humour and Twain-like style comes through in these these editorials.

From the *New Denver Ledge*, January 16, 1896.

"Canada has no quarrel with the United States. We do not envy the Yankees in any way. They have a great country, so have we. They speak English, so do we. They drink water, so do we. They wear pants, so do we. They go to church, so do we. Their blood is red, so is ours. Their ancestors came from Europe, so did ours. Why should Canucks disagree with the Yanks? A family might as well fight among themselves, especially in this part of the Dominion, where the two countries are linked hand in hand in the development of the great mining region on earth. We are all after the gold, silver, and lead, and have no time to quarrel. We admire the Yanks...and trust that every one of them in the

Kootenays will dig up two dollars for a year's interest in this great moral and religious weekly."

Lowery's words were not all well received. The Canadian Pacific Railway refused to carry his papers because of his contrary opinions, his lambasting of the CPR company and his anti-establishment views. He paid for his controversial views, and his fellow editors also commented on Lowery's paper demise. The following clips come from the *Moyie Leader* of Feb 7, 1903.

"*Cranbrook Herald*: In prohibiting Lowery's claim transmission through the mails it may be inferred that the postal authorities are afraid of the naked truth. Lowery should put pajamas on his ideas." And from the *New Denver Ledge*, Lowery's own sarcastic response: "An ozonagram from Sandon states that the parson's dog, which loafs around the Paystreak print works in Sandon, has got appendicitis or something similar. In lieu of liver he swallowed a copy of Lowery's Claim for breakfast, without knowing that its passage through the mail was prohibited."

He also voiced political barbs in his defence, with this piece for the Greenwood Ledge and reprinted in the *Moyie Leader* of Nov 10, 1906.

"If Lemieux would bar Eaton's catalogues out of the mails he would make a host of votes. It is a wonder that somebody with a political pull does not persuade him to do it. He could easily do it upon the grounds that pictures of ladies clothing are indecent and immoral."

F. E. Simpson, editor and publisher of the *Cranbrook Herald* ran a column entitled "Observations By the Old Man". This is his account published in 1906 of Lowery's highs and lows in the newspaper business, a kind of tribute and portrayal of a fellow country editor.

"There are all kinds of newspaper men in the west, but R.T. Lowery, of Lowery's Claim, is about the last of the old type of western journalists who made the country known in the early days when a printing office consisted as a rule, of a bag of type and an army press that could be strapped upon a back of a pack mule and carried many miles in a day over the mountains. Lately Mr. Lowery has been unfortunate. His health has been failing and now the Canadian post office officials have declared that his paper, the Nelson Claim, is unfit for transmission through the mails. Speaking of the man and his future intentions, the Spokane Spokesman Review of recent date says:

"R.T. Lowery- the famous, not to say notorious Lowery- of Lowery's Claim, now published in Nelson,B.C. is soon to become Lowery the peripatetic. His paper will have the unique distinction of being perhaps the only paper in the world with no home and no permanent editorial office.

"Lowery is going on a tramp. In the last little while he has fallen upon evil days Only a week ago the Ishmaelite editor received a severe looking document from the Canadian post office department telling him that he could no longer use the Canadian mails. It was their sense of decency, they said, that prompted this step. Lowery will tell you that it was their prudery and the malice they bore him. Much as he protested, however, the redoubtable R. T. has commenced to send his journal by express lest the postal people tear it up. Now he has decided to go upon the road and will issue his paper from whatever town he may happen to be in at time of going to press.

"He proposes to visit Spokane for a short time, he will call at Seattle, Portland will number him among her citizens; and he mentions San Diego as one of his stops.

"Lowery is one of the only and original boom town editors. He came to the Kootenay district 16 years ago when the prototypes of the Bret Harte tale were beginning to see the possibilities of the Canadian gold fields. After three years he got a few fonts of type and a Washington press and started the Kaslo Claim. To-day such a journal would raise an outcry from half the populace, but in its day the miners were glad to have it at four bits a copy. Lowery foresaw the downfall of the Kaslo boom, and said so; whereupon his life became unsafe and men spoke openly of lynching. In its sixteenth week the Claim perished and Lowery and the "devil" who worked the press got out a farewell issue. On the front page was a tombstone made of printers' rule and over it in huge letters the words BUSTED B'GOSH.

"The unpaid advertisements were turned upside down as a gentle reminder to the delinquents and Lowery jumped the town. He ran the Ledge in Nakusp, the Paystreak in Sandon, the Ledger in Fernie, the Ledge in Rossland, another Claim in Kaslo, the Nugget in Grand Forks, another Claim in Nelson and half a dozen other papers of greater or less note. Now, aged 48, he is in Nelson with the third and last Claim.

"Religion is his bête noir and ministers of the ordinary sort he blacksmiths on all occasions. Now and again there is a risqué story or editorial note and all through the paper are liberal quotations from the nonconformist editors of the continent.

"But Lowery is a sick man. The days when he tried to climb trees on horseback are telling on him. He is seeking the elixir of youth and thinks that in travel he will find it. The Claim will be reduced by half and he will have it printed from the town where he makes his home.

"Strength to his elbow" say the miners, and the clergymen throughout the country are already laying their heads together and whetting the tomahawk as they confer."

The Colonel never married but he did write a bit of a self portrait. The following excerpt from *"Lowery's Claim"*, published in 1902, gives us a taste of his sassy tongue-in-cheek style.

"We have never committed matrimony. Not because we are averse to the touch of a feminine hand, or the delicious caresses that comes from a woman who loves you but simply owing to the fact that we have never had the time nor opportunity to size up the situation that would upset the equilibrium of our placid career. It would revolutionize our entire life. We would have to buy lace curtains, enlarge our bed and sleep in a room decorated with dresses, corsets, petticoats, and other lingerie of the gentler sex. Then we would have to get in early every night without carrying a jag of green onions and milkshakes. It would never do to stumble into our boudoire at 3 a.m. and have our beloved say in a low, sweet, and reproachful voice: 'Colonel, you are slightly jagged'! Such a remark would cause trouble, and consequently for a while longer we will continue to eat onions at night and sleep where no soprano can break the even tenor of our ways."

Sandon the "Silver City"- In 1898, an incorporated city of 5,000 with 24 hotels, 23 saloons, 4 newspapers, a championship hockey team, 3 churches, banks and stores, (not to mention 115 ladies of the evenings!!) with the most advanced electric light and power system in North America at that time." (from an original postcard of Klaus Goedecke)

Like all good storytellers, Lowery wrote of his time and place. The time and place for this story was Sandon, in a time and town that was known as the 'Silvery Slocan'.

"Requiem for a Gambler -
The day Morris Butterman cashed in his chips."

"In 97 there were flush times in the Slocan. The overflow of the Rossland boom swished through the silver camps and coated them with gold. The wash struck Sandon the hardest, and for months that town had its Cairo-like street literally paved with dollars and playing cards. Sandon is built in a gulch between high mountains, o'er which the sun occasionally rubbers the burg. In those days it was a hot locality. All night long the pianos shrieked below the 'dead line' while above it the booze factories had no keys. The clinking of glasses kept time to the rattle of chips and cries of That's good, I'm fat! 'Put in with yo', etc. Those were the days when it cost many a plunk to look at your hole card, and chubbers were under the table. Gamblers were thicker than 'coons at a cake wal', and a flash of sunlight made the lower end of the camp look like a switch-yard with all the danger signals on fire. The camp never closed up. It was one long carnival of cards, wine and women. When one shift went flewey another took its place, and Canada's Monte Carlo never blinked an eye.

"About this time, Morris Butterman hailed camp. Morris had no yellow in him, and packed more than 60 years on his broad back. He had been a gambler for nearly half a century. He had faced the tiger in Montana, shot craps in New Orleans, dealt stud on the old Mississippi and peeped from behind fours in many a draw game. So when he hit the camp he was not afraid of anything in sight. He dealt faro in the Bucket of Blood Saloon and kept his shirt bosom ever white. For a long time his meal ticket had figures on it, and then the splits came. The crash in silver, and then the strike, soon made Sandon look like a dirty deuce in a new deck, and the old gambler went up the hill to cook for a while, but he did not suit and wandered back again, broke, but sad, silent and proud.

"Several of the boys noticed that he did not eat regularly, and proffered him aid, but he shook his head and stayed pat. One day, about five in the afternoon, he passed through the Bucket of Blood to the stairway on the rear to his room. As he mounted the steps he turned and took a long look at the bar and Handsome Jack. Late the next afternoon Jack went upstairs to the old man's room and found him dead. He had put on his best clothes, got under the blankets, took a swallow of poison and cashed in. And thus Morris quit the game- a philosopher. Old, broke, and nothing behind the deal, he preferred to pass up, rather than burden his friends.

"With more time, and a pen trained to run romantic, I could have painted a tale from the last deal in this gambler's life that would have touched many a soul, but I throw it in as we go to press, and let it go as it looks. It's real. Just a dash of tragedy in the fever of mining camp life."

For all of Lowery's wit and intelligence, he had strong opinions against the Chinese. His opinion in favour of increasing the head tax and other issues portray the racist attitudes of the time. Today, his remarks and other opinions against race, religion, and cultural differences would not go unchallenged.

'Old Bill', as the Colonel was affectionately referred to, was a regular at the New Denver hospital. A record book gives us this entry from April 12, 1899. "Dishcharged R.T. Lowery, New Denver. Admitted April 12, 1899. Same Old Thing."

His own words that preface his *"Lowery's Claim"* speak for the man behind the wire-rimmed glasses. From April, 1906:

"Lowery's Claim is devoted to Truth, Humor and Justice, and is published monthly at Nelson, B.C., Canada. It is sent, postpaid, to any part of the world for $1 a year. Advertising rates are $2 an inch each insertion.

"Lowery's Claim has never been raided by the sheriff, railroaded by an indignant populace, nor bulldozed by the brokers who issue tickets on heaven for a consideration. It does not believe in the fall of man, nor the hydra-head-ed god waved before a long-suffering public by those who peddle theologic dope, and subsist upon the fears and superstitions of the human race. It believes in everything good, and hopes that a method will yet be discovered that will smelt all evil out of the world and leave nothing but gold in the heart of man. If you believe as we do send in as many subscribers as possible so that we can keep the press running until a process is discovered that will jar all misery from this universe and annex it to the flower garden in the New Jerusalem. R.T. Lowery, Editor and Financier."

Colonel Lowery died at the age of 62 on May 21, 1921, in the hospital in Grand Forks. The Nelson Branch of the Kootenay Pioneers Association gave him his burial. He was a newspaper man extraordinaire, a champion for the miners of the day and the despair of the nurses who admitted him for the 'same old thing.'

Lowery's style, wit and humor were compared by other newspaper men to Mark Twain and Calgary newspaper man Bob Edwards of the *Calgary Eye Opener*. It seems only fitting to include a short piece by Mark Twain, another man of words, who tells his own story of how he became a writer and newspaper man. A man who set a precedent with his mind, and words, and set a literary and stylistic precedent that influenced writers like Lowery.

Born Samuel Clemens on November 30, 1835 in Florida, Missouri, he claimed the pen name Mark Twain for himself while writing for a Nevada newspaper. He, like Lowery, commented on the events of the day, as they witnessed history unfolding in their midst. The following story shows a poignant and reflective style as Twain remarks on the importance of temperament and circumstance in a person's life, philosophical topics, just as prevalent today as they were more than a century ago.

This is from the story "The Turning-Point of my Life" by Mark Twain. (Excerpted from *Great Short Works of Mark Twain*)

"To me, the most important feature of my life is its literary feature. I have been professionally literary something more than forty years. There have been many turning-points in my life, but the one that was the last link in the chain appointed to conduct me to the literary guild is the most *conspicuous* link in that chain. *Because* it was the last one. It was not any more important than its predecessors. All the other links have an inconspicuous look, except the crossing of the Rubicon; but as factors in making me literary they are all of the one size, the crossing of the Rubicon included.

"I know how I came to be literary, and I will tell the steps that led up to it and brought it about.

"The crossing of the Rubicon was not the first one, it was hardly even a recent one; I should have to go back ages before Caesar's day to find the first one. To save space I will go back only a couple of generations and start with an incident of my boyhood. When I was twelve and a half years old, my father died. It was in the spring. The summer came, and brought with it an epidemic of measles. For a time, a child died almost every day. The village was paralyzed with fright, distress, despair. Children that were not smitten with the disease were imprisoned in their homes to save them from the infection. In the homes there were no cheerful faces, there was no music, there was no singing but of solemn hymns, no voice but of prayer, no romping was allowed, no noise, no laughter, the family moved spectrally about on tiptoe, in a ghostly hush. I was a prisoner. My soul was steeped in this awful dreariness and in fear. At some time or other every day and every night a sudden shiver shook me to the marrow, and I said to myself, "There, I've got it! And I shall die." Life on these miserable terms was not worth living, and at last I made up my mind to get the disease and have it over, one way or the other. I escaped from the house and went to the house of a neighbor where a playmate of mine was very ill with the malady. When the chance offered I crept into his room and got into bed with him. I was discovered by his mother and sent back to captivity. But I had the disease; they could not take that from me. I came near dying. The whole village was interested, and anxious, and sent for news of me every day; and not only once a day, but several times. Everybody believed I would die; but on the fourteenth day a change came for the worse and they were disappointed.

"This was a turning-point of my life. (Link number one.) For when I got well my mother closed my school career and apprenticed me to a printer. She was tired of trying to keep me out of mischief, and the adventure of the measles decided her to put me into more masterful hands than hers.

"I became a printer, and began to add one link after another to the chain which was to lead me into the literary profession. A long road, but I could not know that; and as I did not know what its goal was, or even that it had one, I was indifferent. Also contented.

"A young printer wanders around a good deal, seeking and finding work; and seeking again, when necessity commands. N.B. Necessity is a *Circumstance*; Circumstance is man's master- and when Circumstance commands, he must *obey*; he may argue the matter- that is his privilege, just as it is the honorable privilege of a falling body to argue with the attraction of gravitation- but it won't do any good, he must obey. I wandered for ten years, under the guidance and dictatorship of Circumstance, and finally arrived in a city of Iowa, where I worked several months. Among the books that interested me in those days was one about the Amazon. The traveler told an alluring tale of his long voyage up the great river from Para to the sources of the Madeira, through the heart of an enchanted land, a land wastefully rich in tropical wonders, a romantic land where all the birds and flowers and animals were of the museum varieties, and where the alligator and the crocodile and the monkey seemed as much at home as if they were in the Zoo. Also, he told an astonishing tale about *coca*, a vegetable product of miraculous powers, asserting that it was so nourishing and so strength-giving that the natives of the mountains of the Madeira region would tramp up hill and down all day on a pinch of powdered coca and require no other sustenance.

"I was fired with a longing to ascend the Amazon. Also with a longing to open up a trade in coca with all the world. During months I dreamed that dream, and tried to contrive ways to get to Para, and spring that splendid enterprise upon an unsuspecting planet. But all in vain. A person may *plan* as much as he wants to, but nothing of consequence is likely to come of it until the magician *Circumstance* steps in and takes the matter off his hands. At last Circumstance came to my help. It was in this way. Circumstance, to help or hurt another man, made him lose a fifty-dollar bill in the street; and to help or hurt me, made me find it. I advertised the find, and left for the Amazon the same day. This was another turning-point, another link.

"Could Circumstance have ordered another dweller in that town to go to the Amazon and open up a world-trade in coca on a fifty-dollar basis and been obeyed? No, I was the only one. There were other fools there—shoals and shoals of them—but they were not of my kind. I was the only one of my kind.

"Circumstance is powerful, but it cannot work alone; it has to have a partner, Its partner is man's *temperament* – his natural disposition. His temperament is not his invention, it is *born* in him, and he has no authority over it, neither is he responsible for its acts. He cannot change it, nothing can change it, nothing can modify it—except temporarily. But it won't stay modified. It is permanent, like the color of the man's eyes and the shape of his ears. Blue eyes are gray in certain unusual lights; but they resume their natural color when that stress is removed.

"A Circumstance that will never coerce one man will have no effect upon a man of a different temperament. It Circumstance had thrown the bank-note in Caesar's way, his temperament would not have made him start for the Amazon. His temperament would have compelled him to do something with the money, but not that. It might have made him advertise the note—and *wait*. We can't tell. Also, it might have made him go to New York and buy into the Government, with results that would leave Tweed nothing to learn when it came his turn.

"Very, well, Circumstance furnished the capital, and my temperament told me what to do with it. Sometimes a temperament is an ass. When that is the case the owner of it is an ass, too, and is going to remain one. Training, experience, association, can temporarily so polish him, improve him, exalt him that people will think he is a mule, but they will be mistaken. Artificially he *is* a mule, for the time being, but at bottom he is an ass yet, and will remain one.

"By temperament I was the kind of person that *does* things. Does them, and reflects afterward. So I started for the Amazon without reflecting and without asking any questions. That was more than fifty years ago. In all that time my temperament has not changed, by even a shade. I have been punished many and many a time, and bitterly, for doing things and reflecting afterward, but these tortures have been of no value to me: I still do the thing commanded by Circumstance and Temperament, and reflect afterward. Always violently. When I am reflecting, on those occasions, even deaf persons can hear me think.

"I went by the way of Cincinnati, and down the Ohio and Mississippi. My idea was to take ship, at New Orleans, for Para. In New Orleans I inquired, and found there was no ship leaving for Para. Also, that there never had *been* one leaving for Para. I reflected. A policeman came and asked me what I was doing, and I told him. He made me move on, and said if he caught me reflecting in the public street again he would run me in.

"After a few days I was out of money. Then Circumstance arrived, with another turning-point of my life— a new link. On my way down, I had made the acquaintance of a pilot. I begged him to teach me the river, and he consented. I became a pilot.

"By and by Circumstance came again—introducing the Civil War, this time, in order to push me ahead another stage or two toward the literary profession. The boats stopped running, my livelihood was gone.

"Circumstance came to the rescue with a new turning-point and a fresh new link, My brother was appointed secretary to the new Territory of Nevada, and he invited me to go with him and help in his office, I accepted.

"In Nevada, Circumstance furnished me the silver fever and I went into the mines to make a fortune, as I supposed; but that was not the idea. The idea was to advance me another step toward literature. For amusement, I scribbled things for the Virginia City *Enterprise*. One isn't a printer for ten years without setting up acres of good and bad literature, and learning—unconsciously at first, consciously later —to discriminate between the two, within his mental limitations; and meantime he is unconsciously acquiring what is called a "style." One of my efforts attracted attention, and the *Enterprise* sent for me and put me on its staff.

"And so I became a journalist—another link. By and by Circumstance and the Sacramento *Union* sent me to the Sandwich Islands for five or six months, to write up sugar. I did it; and threw in a good deal of extraneous mater that hadn't anything to do with sugar. But it was this extraneous matter that helped me to another link.

"It made me notorious, and San Francisco invited me to lecture. Which I did, And profitably. I had long had a desire to travel and see the world, and now Circumstance had most kindly and unexpectedly hurled me upon the platform and furnished me the means. So I joined the "Quaker City Excursion."

"When I returned to America, Circumstance was waiting on the pier—with the *last* link- the conspicuous, the consummating, the victorious link; I was asked to *write a book*, and I did it, and called it *The Innocents Abroad*. Thus I became a member of the literary guild. That was forty-two years ago, and I have been a member ever since. Leaving the Rubicon incident away back where it belongs, I can say with truth that the reason I am in the literary profession is because I had the measles when I was twelve years old."

Mark Twain was a prolific writer and is probably best known for his novels *Tom Sawyer* and *Adventures of Huckleberry Finn* as well as numerous short stories. He died at the age of 74 on April 21, 1910.

Lowery might have taken a page out of Mark Twain, for it was circumstance and temperament that kept him going in his pursuit of voicing his opinions of the day.

BOB EDWARDS –THE "EYE-OPENER"

R.C. " Bob" Edwards, Calgary, Alberta (ca.1915)
Glenbow Archives (NA-937-12)

Edwards was born Robert Chambers Edwards in Edinburgh, Scotland, on September 12, 1864. He arrived in the United States in 1884, and by 1897 started up the *Wetaskiwin Free Lance*. He launched the *Eye Opener* on March 4, 1902 from High River, Alberta. He came up with the name *Eye Opener*, thinking few could resist subscribing to a paper with that name. Clashes with the church and the establishment forced him to move the paper to Calgary. He exposed the hypocrisy of the church, and expressed his views in support of prostitutes. He was ahead of his time, and argued for old age pensions, minimum wage laws, travelling libraries and school books with Canadian content. He was a whistle blower against the establishment and he printed what he thought was right. Like Lowery, he battled with the courts for his controversial views and political barbs and had a personal battle with booze. He was known for creating characters with names like Albert Buzzard Cholomondoley of Skookingham and Peter J. McGonigle through whom he voiced his anti- upper- crust opinions. Many of his readers believed these were real people. He wrote well and plenty on the subject of booze and on the hypocrisy of society and the prohibition laws. His writing was the platform for his opinions and casts a reflection of the world at the time. Fred Smyth had this to say about him in his paper, the "*Moyie Leader*" of April 28, 1911.

"Bob Edwards will shortly move the 'Eye Opener' back to Calgary. Edwards has tried Toronto, Winnipeg, and Fort William, but somehow the paper never took as well in the east as it did in the west. The easterners seemed to be afraid of the naked truth, and Edwards never saw fit to clothe his ideas in pajamas."

Edward's sense of humour and original style come through in this short piece on the downfalls of booze, excerpted from the book, *The Best of Bob Edwards,* by Hugh Dempsey.

"Booze is a bad thing when it is aboozed. Used in small quantities it is harmless enough. The difficulty lies in using it in small quantities. With those who have a constitutional tendency towards liquor one drink means two, and two means a drunk. Therefore those who, as is often the case, have hereditary tendencies in this direction should abstain altogether. The pernicious stuff will catch them napping at last.

"One thing our benevolent government might do is this. They should make the inspectors do a little more to earn their salaries. It should be part of their duties to appear unexpectedly at the various hotels in their district and make a thorough attest of the spirituous liquors sold over the bar. This, I gambel, would bring forth some startling revelations. Barney Cooper's first official test of bulk whiskey would read 'Muriatic acid one quarter, alcohol one eight, fusel oil one eight, fish-hooks one quarter, alcohol one eight, strychnine one eight.' Think of pouring that mixture down your epiglottis fifteen or twenty times a day, trying to make yourself believe that you are having a good time. It is a fool's paradise.

"The result? Sore heads, shattered nerves, empty pockets, and worst of all, the loss of the friendship and respect of good men and women. It is the vendor of the booze that wears the diamonds. Once in the maelstrom it is hard to get out, for there is no gainsaying that the booze-life has its fascinations. One hears bright conversations at the bar and some very pretty wit is occasionally slung around. Things are looked at from the roseate point of view. They remain roseate till the following morning, when it takes three or four fish-hook cocktails to get back to par. This is the thorn. Better to eschew the beastly stuff altogether. Don't do as I do; do as I tell you.

"I do not believe in that most impracticable piece of legislative nonsense that goes by the name of prohibition. Where prohibition exists the people drink spirits almost exclusively, because it is easier handled by the vendors. Those who formerly drank light lager have to slop up some villainous concoction which they regard as sweet because it is stolen fruit. Make the procuring of booze as easy as possible and there will be less booze drunk. Give every responsible man who has a hotel which complies with the statute a license. The revenues will be increased without any additional drunkenness. A man has only so much to spend on booze anyhow and will spend that much if there are one or twenty bars in his town.

"My advice to beginners is to leave it alone altogether, even beer and light wines. In the case of socially inclined young men indulgence in these harmless beverages too often degenerates into a craving for the fish-hooks. The whole traffic only breeds sorrow and ought to be sidestepped.

"Temperance is corporal piety. It is the preservation of divine order in the body and diffuses through its innermost recesses a healthful spirit which has no fish-hooks in it."

Edward's humourous style and creative bent is again seen in this piece, featuring one of his fictional characters, through whom he spoke, excerpted from *The Best of Bob Edwards*.

"The Pan-Boozological Congress of Demented Bartenders was held in Winnipeg this year and met in session last week at the Royal Alexandra.

Mr. Peter J. McGonigle, the distinguished journalist of Midnapore, who was on his way home after taking the jag cure at Port Arthur, was invited to be present and address the delegates. This he kindly consented to do, and in the course of the morning prepared a thoughtful address on "The Horrors of Square Gin." Being unused to public speaking, Mr. McGonigle nerved himself for the ordeal by slipping round to the bar before the proceedings commenced and throwing three or four stiff old hookers into himself. He argued that one little flurry of rye would not materially affect the good results of his recent cure.

"There may be some here who prefer Square Face to Old Tom and it is far from my intention, I assure you, to wound the susceptibilities of any one by lauding one kind of gin to the detriment of another. When a booze artist of average intelligence regards his past life he has food for thought. Having partaken of that food, he has to take several horns to wash it down, and so the world wags on. (Applause) We all have our good points, but so has a paper of pins. (Laughter)

"The main cause of drunkenness, Mr. Chairman, in this Canada of ours, is the pathetic tendency most booze-fighters have to taking six drinks before breakfast instead of two. I should like to see some form of legislation introduced whereby it became a crime to take more than two snifters before breakfast, (Hear, Hear!) When a man imbibes, say three Collinses on an empty stomach he gets laid out too soon, having probably to retire to the hay before ten o'clock. Thus your receipts are curtailed for the day and the boss thinks you are knocking down. (A voice, 'That's so!') On the other hand, let your honest booze-fighter confine himself to a couple of snorts in the early morn, just to get the bugs out of his eyes, and then let him make a beeline for the dining room and stuff himself full of ham-and. What must be the natural result, my friends, of such wise policy? That man will last all day and well into the night. (Loud and prolonged applause.)

"Such a concerted movement on the part of the vast horde of rotgut guzzlers would make the wheels of your great and noble industry move the faster, would hasten the filling of your cash distilleries, spread happiness amongst the hotelkeepers, add to the prosperity of the medical profession, fill your hospitals with paying patients, promote the interests of the calomel and bromide merchants, increase the welfare of every gravedigger in the land and cause the marts of the world to hum with the sound of popping corks to the end that the eternal gaiety of nations might not be dimmed by the disgraceful efforts of those who too lightly claim that Adam's ale is more conducive to longevity than Seagram's rye. (Frantic applause, many of the delegates jumping up and waving their hankerchiefs.)

"The economic value of booze is incalculable. Why, for instance, should you pay six bits to go and see the menagerie attached to a circus, when with the simple aid of three bottles of square gin and two Scotch you can see a far more various and curious collection of animals, and none of them in cages either!

You do not even have to leave your place of abode to view them. They come right up to you. (Cheers.)

"Mr. Chairman, I go west tonight. I shall take with me the message to Midnapore that the Pan-Boozological Congress of Demented Bartenders is solid for the unity of the Empire. (Tremendous applause) I shall convey to the Midnapore board of trade, which consists of myself, my assistant, the local hardware merchant and four cowpunchers, that your congress has declared itself resolutely in favor of free trade in agricultural implements and reciprocity with the United States. I shall tell them that while favoring free trade, you look with grave disfavor on free drinks."

Edwards' Scottish education in philosophy, classical literature, logic and metaphysics would provide him with his intellectual backbone. Bob Edwards wrote on a variety of subjects. He created his own "Society Notes," medical advice column and cooking hints, all with artistic license to contrast the high society pages.

His short pieces on society reveal his sarcastic wit about men and women. Excerpted from *The Best of Bob Edwards*.

"A man likes a good cook *before* dinner. But after he has eaten his tomato soup he doesn't want a hard-working woman to come around him, tired out, with her hair in a tangle and her eyes and face red from peeling onions and standing over a hot fire. He wants some light fluffy creature, with the chiffon and lace and all the rest of it, who doesn't know an eggbeater from a carpet sweeper."

Edwards also created his own cooking columns— a satiric response to the proper ways and the opposite of any high style glossiness of so called proper etiquette. Here is a sample called "How To Cook Things" that ran in the *Crag and Canyon*, August 02, 1902.

"Onion Salad- Get one good strong onion and kill it. Get a hammer and a nail and drive the smell out of it. Soak it in kerosene oil two seconds, boil de onion in the oven. Pour de salad over de onion undil id resolves.

"Shortcake- Get a small boy to pick two quards off berries. Roll de berries mid a rolling pin. Add de juice of seven lemons. Take von cub off oatmeal and a pocketful mitt rye flour. Stir mid a lead pencil— No. 2. Cook id until it gets to a sealskin brown. Burn de bottom off de cake a little.

"Take four bound off cranulated sugar van spoonful mit flour. Bake two eggs loose and take de yolks of de eggs. Pour in three or four good sized small sponges. Stuff dem mit milk, eat slowly.

"Lemoncake—Take de yolks off five lemons, beat dem until dey was plack and plue. Grade in won quard of nitmegs, wash off one pind of milk and pud did in; add von bar soap; put in von fried oranges; lit id remain until id begins to ged ripe. Leave id in de oven till you take it out.

"Mincepie—Get von piece of rubber and cut de undercrust; scallop der edges mit der shears; buy four rounds off cow's neck; chop up one peck off apples, basket and all. Add von yard of red flannel and a peck of sawdust. Give it two coats of varnish. Cook id one hour and sixteen inches."

Edwards had much to say on a variety of topics. The following shows that the use of the right or the wrong word can mean the difference between flattery or flagrant criticism. Here are some of his witty remarks on the sexes, excerpted again from *The Best of Bob Edwards.*

"Call a girl a chick and she smiles; call a woman a hen and she howls. Call a young woman a witch and she is pleased; call an old woman a witch and she is indignant. Call a girl a kitten and she rather likes it; call a woman a cat and she hates you. Women are queer.

"If you call a man a gay dog it will flatter him; call him a pup, a hound, or a cur and he will try to alter the map of your face. He doesn't mind being called a bull or a bear, yet he will object to being mentioned as a calf or a cub. Men are queer, too."

Edwards stood up for the common man and voiced his opinions on war, injustice, fraud, hypocrisy and everything in between.

The following piece reveals Edwards' plea for peace and respect for all, and in it we see the man, R.C. "Bob" Edwards, behind these words in "The Outcast's Prayer", published in the *Calgary Eye Opener*, Feb 26, 1916.

"Almighty God, All-powerful God, we come to thee to rectify some of the great evils that exist in this old world thou hast created, and to remove the causes of misery, starvation, privation, degredation, and poverty, in the land of the free and the home of the brave. Oh, Lord, have mercy on the millions of working men that are being butchered every day in Christian Europe, for every war is a rich man's war and a poor man's fight. In times of peace our stomachs yearn for a beefsteak. In times of war we are filled with bullets. And, Oh Lord, we ask thee to stop this useless murdering of innocent men.

"Let those who declare war do the fighting. Let those Champagne-Guzzling, Bleary-Eyed, Bald-Headed Plutocrats fight their own battles. If they want blood, let them shed their own blood.

"Oh Lord, deliver us from the greed and graft that exists in this nation and form the parasites who neither toil nor spin, but bedeck their persons with finery until they glitter in the gleaming like a rotten dog salmon afloat in the moonlight.

"Oh, wonderful God, deliver us! We are blessed with preachers who draw fat salaries. Men pray to you to send heaven on earth, and the rest of the week dare you to do it. Verily, our institutions are badly mixed, for we have Bible houses, bawdy houses, barrel houses and breweries. Oh Lord, help us, for we have criminals, paupers and hordes of industrial cannibals whom we call business men, professors who draw their salary and convictions from the same source. Oh Lord, merciful God, we have thieves, theologians, Christians and confidence men; also priests, prisons, politicians and poverty; convents, convicts, scabs and scallywags; traces of virtue and tons of vice. We have trusts and tramps, money and misery, homes and hunger, salvation and soup, and psalms sung by hypocrites in an organized bummery who expect us to pave their way to heaven by begging old pants, coats and hats and in thy name sell them to the poor, thereby spreading disease and vermin to multiply.

"Protect us, Oh Lord, and deliver us, for the groceries association hold us up, while poverty holds us down. Some of our butchers put embalming fluid on purtrified beef, for they know that it would not stink and the unsuspecting public would not eat it without belching. Deliver us from those who make canned beef out of sick cows, mules and horses, and corpses of those who eat it, and may the price of hamburger, beef stews, waffles and holey doughnuts come down and our wages come up to meet them, and may we be permitted to fill up on those luxuries three times a day, for to be without them causes great pain in our gastric region.

"And, Oh Lord, we do not understand why poodle dogs have private baths and are attended by maids and valets, are shampooed, manicured and kissed, fed on choice steaks and drink cream, while thousands of little children make after your own image, live off garbage cans. Christ never said, suffer little poodle dogs to come unto me; and Oh Lord, may the society women cease to give their affections to poodle dogs instead of to babies.

"And, Oh Lord, we ask thee to have mercy on the blanket stiffs, such as rail-roaders, loggers, muckers and skinners, and may they be permitted to make at least seven dollars and six bits before they get fired, and may their mulligans be of better class and contain no more old shoes, gum-boots and scrap-iron, and may their blankets rest lightly on their blistered backs and contain no insects that might discommode them.

"May the farmer plant his spuds more closely to the railroad track, and his chickens roam more closely to the jungles, and we will ever be grateful to the all powered God.

In a Special Edition published May 5, 1917, the voice of Bob Edwards reveals itself in this piece: "The Man Behind the Calgary Eye Opener."

"Lord let me keep a straight way in the path of honor;
And a straight face in the presence of solemn asses'
Let me not truckle to the high, nor bull doze low;
Let me frolic with the Jack and the Joker and now and
 then win the game; lead me unto truth and beauty
 and tell me her name; keep me sane but not too sane,
let me condemn no man because of grammar, and no
woman because of her morals, neither being responsible
for either. Preserve my sense of honor and values
and proportions. Let me be healthy while I live, but not live too
long. Which is about all for today, Lord. Amen."

Bob Edwards published his last issue of the *Eye Opener* on July 29, 1922. He died at the age of fifty-eight, on November 14, 1922. He left a legacy of humour.

NORMAN LUXTON-
BANFF'S 'BOOSTER' EXTRAORDINAIRE

Stereoscopic portraits of Norman Luxton 1905
Whyte Museum of the Canadian Rockies (Lux B 1-14)

Norman Luxton was many things: an entrepreneur, collector, taxidermist, newspaperman, adventurer and promoter. Not known for his writing style per se, Luxton's name would be ultimately linked to the town of Banff.

Norman Kenny Luxton was born into a family of newspapermen. His father, William Fisher Luxton, founded the *Manitoba Free Press* which later became the *Winnipeg Free Press*. Luxton was born in Winnipeg in 1877. In 1895 he came to Calgary and worked for the *Calgary Herald* as a reporter and bill collector. Norman Luxton left Calgary and was 20 years old and looking for adventure when he met a Danish born captain by the name of John Voss in Vancouver. In 1901, he set out with Captain Voss to navigate the world. The voyage for him was ill-fated. The captain and Luxton had a fiery relationship and were at odds with each other and in Luxton's words "after washing overboard and clinging for my life on a corral reef near Fiji, I was forced to terminate my foolhardy adventure, while Captain Voss did eventually circumnavigate the world." (Excerpted from the exhibition, The Stuff of Legend: The Luxton Family in Banff and the Bow Valley, Whyte Museum of the Canadian Rockies)

After his voyage with Voss, he returned to Calgary 100 pounds lighter. Friends convinced him to spend time at Brett's Sanitarium in Banff. It was temperament and circumstance that would propel the life of this man and link it with so many things at the forefront of history, as his following words will portray. "I meant to stay in Banff a few weeks, but I liked it so awfully well that I stayed 60 years." (Excerpted from The Stuff of Legend: The Luxton family in Banff and the Bow Valley, Whyte Museum of the Canadian Rockies)

"In 1902, I rented a dilapidated printing office and was soon producing the *Crag and Canyon*. All the local merchants advertised in it, including the Banff Springs Hotel and the Parks Department. I once made a bet with the Parks Commissioner that any improvements he had done for Banff were suggested by my paper first. He sent a man to go over the files for a week, and he had to admit that he lost the bet.

"Ottawa was getting more and more despotic each year regarding government of Banff. Orders in Council were being thrown at us like a breakfast menu; people's birthrights through their homesteads were being exchanged for forty-year leases. I convinced Sir James Lougheed, then Minister of the Interior, that the people should elect an advisory board of Banff citizens. It helped put a stop to the autocratic government of Ottawa and the heavy hand of Parks Commissioner, J.B. Harkin.

We all built Banff in spite of the fact that the government owned the damned place."

In 1902 he took over the *Crag and Canyon* and was at the helm of that paper until 1951. He was at the forefront of history and he had Banff as his expose. He was the ultimate booster, a man who wanted his town to make it. He championed the possibilities as Banff as a winter resort highlighting winter activities. He also was responsible for showcasing Aboriginal sports and the way of life and handicrafts of the Stoney and other native tribes. In these words he shows himself as entrepreneur and promoter of "Banff the Beautiful". (Excerpted from The Stuff of Legend: the Luxton Family in Banff and the Bow Valley — Whyte Museum of the Canadian Rockies)

"It worried me that Banff had no hotel that was open year round. Its only connection to the outside world was the daily trains running east and west. Inside three years, I had a stopping place called the King Edward with some 40 rooms and a liquor license. At its opening reception, I threw away the keys, and thus opened Banff's 24-hour-a-day, year round hotel. I also offered all diversions of pleasure for summer guests-tally-ho and buggy trips on the early park roads, trips into the mountains by packhorse, Lake Minnewanka boat tours and a sightseeing pamphlet called Banff the Beautiful, which preceded anything the Parks Department put out by several years." His pamphlet advertised Banff as "Fifty Switzerlands in One" and a "veritable fairyland in winter".

Two events that Luxton was hugely responsible for were Banff's Winter Carnival and Banff's Indian Days. On convincing others to promote winter activities in Banff he wrote the following. (Excerpted from the The Stuff of Legend).

"There was little going on in Banff that I did not have a finger in. The Rotary came to town and I was a charter member. With my membership in the Calgary Board of Trade, hardly a month went by that I was not trying to sell them something of Banff, and so they called me Mr. Banff. I promoted Banff as "The Playground of the Canadian Rockies." In 1906, I published the booklet *Fifty Switzerlands in One —Banff the Beautiful*, which I distributed all over the world.

"In 1909 I convinced Barney Collison, Banff's Stipendiary Magistrate that the citizens of Banff were howling their heads off for winter sports and that he had to wire Ottawa to contribute. The Parks Department agreed to back the Carnival with $500 of labour and ice. That started the Banff Winter Carnival, which became a tremendous advertisement for Banff and its winter possibilities.

I also approached Frank Oliver, Minister of the Interior, and won the concession for the Indian racetrack and campgrounds that have been used ever since, organizing Banff Indian Days into the greatest publicity stunt Banff has ever seen."

Luxton's vision and instincts were right, of course, as today Banff is truly one of the world's most famous playgrounds for winter and summer sports. Luxton had a deep respect for the Stoney Indians and it was again largely due to his promotional skills and encouragement that Banff Indian Days were celebrated in Banff. The *Crag and Canyon* of 1934 ran this column promoting the event.

"Indian Days Are Here Once More."

"A tableau depicting Indian chieftains vested in stately raiment signally enhanced by symbolic eagle feathers, medicine men, braves, and squaws, bedecked in colourful apparel suited to their station, stirred with the breath of life as the gaily caparisoned steeds of hundreds of Indians marched up Banff Avenue this morning in the opening parade of the three-day revival of Indian lore. This epic of the aborigines of Western Canada forms the 45th link in the annual pageants of the erstwhile rulers of a continent who, for three days, resume kingship of the domain they once surveyed. The escort of the Mounted Police revived memories of early strifes of days long past when the first pale face settlers, imbued with pioneering spirit sought protection as they invaded the plains and mountains for the expansion for a now annexed realm. The Indian Days are made possible through the support of the Canadian Pacific Banff Springs Hotel, merchants and citizens of Banff, the gate receipts, and the untiring efforts of N.K. Luxton and J.I. Brewster who prepare early in the season for novel additions to the program. The hearty co-operation of the Morley tribe is shown in the months they spend with untiring ardor, in preparing their wares, buckskin shirts and vests, beaded moccasins, beadwork of all kinds which receive painstaking attention at the deft hands of the squaws. When the long trek from Morley and Nordegg is completed, the entire Stony tribe pitch their village of tepees under the steep cliffs of Stony Chief Mountain, so named by their ancestors, but re-christened Cascade Mountain by the white man. The village is located at the Banff Race Track at Animal Paddock where events are held each afternoon, tomorrow's program consisting of half and one mile dashes, half-mile squaw race, democrat and harness race, Indian cowboy race, wrestling on horseback, and a bucking contest. Two money prizes will be given for each event."

Georgina Luxton, Hector Crawler, Norman Luxton, Mrs. Hector Crawler, at Banff Indian Days ca. 1915. Byron Harmon, Whyte Museum of the Canadian Rockies (V263/NA 3350)

Banff Indian days showcased Indian lore and their way of life, rituals, legends, handicrafts and sports. Luxton's views on the establishment that didn't support these promotions of Banff were met with editorials like this one in the *Crag and Canyon* of July 24, 1915. " Banff Indian day is slowly but surely becoming world wide known, and while it is hard for the average Banff citizen to see this wonderful day through the eyes of the visiting tourist, there is no one who is not aware of the immense value these two days are to Banff as an advertisement medium.

"It seems that only one institution in the whole Park lack or care little how this day may start or end. Such was not the case in the days of Manager Mathews of the C.P.R. as often out of their private purse Mr. and Mrs. Mathews donated large cash presents to help the days expenses through.

"Last year the big C.P.R. hotel saw fit to refuse the sale of Indian post cards in their building go up especially for Indian day, though it was explained that all money went to the Indians. This year the manager of the hotel Mr. Hempstead could not find time to wish the Indians good-day and this paper wishes to impress on any mortal that can't show a little loyalty to Banff and its interests will never find fault or complaint for not receiving just and honest criticism in the columns of Crag and Canyon."

Luxton was made honorary chief both by the Stoney and the Blackfoot for his support and endeavours.

Luxton's other seminal vision, in the early days of Banff, was to promote Banff as a winter resort. After several years of promoting 'Banff the Beautiful' and the pleasures of winter sports in a Canadian National Park, the announcement of Banff as a Winter Resort was a reality. His exhuberant remarks are evident in this editorial, from the *Crag and Canyon*, February 12, 1910.

"For three or four years past all sorts of talking, pressure and wire-pulling have been brought to bear on the Government and the Canadian Pacific Railway Company to boost Banff along for a winter resort. Those interested were about to drop their tails in despair, for apparently little or no encouragement was given them. Suddenly out of the dark horizon there loom up two mighty personages, whose lights grow brighter as their messages are known—Mr. Hayter Reed, head of the C.P.R. hotel system, and Mr. Howard Douglas, Commissionar of Parks. The former paid the government a call the other day, and so far as is known the winter resort project will be carried to fruition both by the railway company and the Government. If the present ideas are carried out, the Government will build a toboggan slide at least two or three miles in length. A larger skating rink will be operated and curling rinks for visitors' use will be made, while ski-ing, ice-boating and a winter trotting track will all receive attention.

"That Banff will be a success as a winter resort goes without saying. Where in America or Europe can be found more natural resources than in the Canadian National Park? Imagine a toboggan slide starting somewhere above the Corkscrew on Tunnel Mountain, following the course of the drive road to the

Falls, turning there to shoot down on the river towards the bridge. Imagine, again, the fleet of iceboats that could be operated on Lake Minnewanka, 20 miles long and five miles wide. Already a small fleet of nine sails on the lake, and a more exciting and healthy sport cannot be found. Dr. Harry Brett, James Brewster, Jack Standly, and Walter Spicer are the lucky owners of these racers, and from present indications there will be 20 boats next winter instead of nine. Ski-ing, snowshoeing, skating, curling and bob sleighing are winter sports well cultivated in Banff already. The Banff Curling Club is noted for possessing the most picturesque rink in the Canadian West. The Banff Snowshoe Club meets twice a week and over the steaming pot of coffee, around the big camp fire, many stories are told and jolly songs sung. Away up some secluded ravine, or under the precipitous sides of the mountains this club takes the enjoyment that only snowshoers know.

"An extra gay month during each winter will be arranged on similar lines to that which has made a name for Montreal throughout the world.

"Inducements will be offered to horsemen to hold a meet in Banff. Only those who have speeded on a river course know what pleasures are derived from the ice and snow course.

"Skating, curling and sleigh-riding of the very best can be had; unlimited skating on the rivers and lakes, as miles of ice is often free of snow for weeks of the season, and when the snow comes it is no great trouble to keep the snow cleared for a ¼- mile stretch up the river.

"Then, again, the greatest novelty of all is offered the visitors, that of taking a bath in the hot sulphur springs in the open air. On suggesting this to the visitor when the thermometer is around zero, he is inclined to think someone is crazy. But just come to Banff once and see how the inhabitants enjoy the winter. No weather is too cold for a bath in the springs; no mountain side too steep for the daring skier. Each individual in Banff, even to the smallest, finds pleasure there that no other place in the world could give.

"The ladies hockey team is already famous, having vanquished all who ever came before them. The Senior and Junior Clubs never turn down a challenge, and Banff curlers are ready to meet players from any part and have shown themselves doughty knights of the broom, in many a hard-fought game."

Luxton and others who saw Banff's promise as a winter resort saw their promotional and editorial efforts finally pay off as Banff became the winter playground for the citizens of Banff and the destination for others worldwide. Banff's Winter Carnival was another event that showcased Banff as a winter destination, one that showcased winter sports and the revelry of those that participated in the red- cheeked activities of the outdoors. The Banff Winter Carnival was celebrated every year from 1917 and featured an ice palace, a carnival queen, dog-sled races, snowshoe races and figure skating.

Luxton was also an entrepreneur and in 1903 he opened Banff's Indian Trading Store.

" In 1903, I opened the Sign of the Goat Trading Post. I made it look like a museum so that people would be interested, even if they didn't always buy. A few years later, we reopened on the other side of the river, where it stands to this day. In 1927 I renamed it Banff's Indian Trading Store. With my brother Lou, managing the store, we shipped furs, big game heads, Indian beadwork and relics of all kinds everywhere in the world to royalty, millionaires, hunters and tourists.

"I used to keep a pet bear chained to the front of the store, a sure drawing card for eastern city-slickers looking for a piece of the Wild West.

"While many of the Indian curios, our most popular merchandise, were obtained from companies in the United States and eastern Canada, I also traded with the Stoney and Sarcee Indians who made crafts for us to sell."(Excerpted from The Stuff of Legend: Luxton Family in Banff and the Bow Valley- Whyte Museum of the Canadian Rockies)

Norman Luxton married Georgina McDougall in 1904. The McDougall Family also left a legacy to the history of Banff. Luxton died at the age of 86. He published the *Crag and Canyon* for 49 years and left Banff a legacy in words and deeds. He deservedly earned the title of " Mr. Banff." He was a quintessential booster extraordinaire for his town and the times. His daughter, Eleanor Luxton, followed in her father's footsteps and continued the Luxton legacy. The Whyte Museum of The Canadian Rockies in Banff, Alberta, launched a new exhibit in 2009 that was a tribute to Norman K. Luxton and the McDougall Family. The exhibition was called "The Stuff of Legend: The Luxton Family in Banff and the Bow Valley." Luxton was a renowned taxidermist and trained several others who would gain notoriety in this field. He also appeared in a film promoting Banff Indian Days in 1916 and in a Hollywood film shot in Banff in 1941. He deservedly earned the name of Mr. Banff and was a booster extraordinaire for the town he so loved. Who knows if Banff would be what it is today without the likes of Norman Luxton who by circumstance and temperament changed the course of history.

It is these men of ink who have given us snapshots of history, with all the prejudices and opinions of the past. The language of the times may be different than words used today, but the human element is universal. Without these men of ink and their presses and fonts, these glimpses of the past would not exist.

Let us hope that circumstance and temperament will produce other comparable minds and wit to comment on today.

Resources

Whyte Museum of the Canadian Rockies, Banff, Alberta
Eleanor Luxton Historical Foundation, Banff, Alberta
The Stuff of Legend: The Luxton Family in Banff and the Bow Valley, exhibition 2009/2010, Whyte Museum of the Canadian Rockies
Crag and Canyon Newspapers, Whyte Museum archives
Cranbrook Herald, Cranbrook Courier, Daily Townsman newspapers, Cranbrook Historical Archives
Come with me to Yesterday series by D.A. Macdonald and Dave Kay Archives, Canadian Museum of Rail Travel
Canadian Museum of Rail Travel, Cranbrook, British Columbia
Family History Library, Church of Latter Day Saints, Cranbrook, British Columbia
Sandon Historical Society, New Denver, British Columbia
Silvery Slocan Museum, New Denver, British Columbia
Silverton Historical Association, Silverton, British Columbia
Glenbow Museum Archives, Calgary, Alberta
Cranbrook Public Library, Cranbrook, British Columbia
Moyie Leader newspapers, Moyie High House Museum, Moyie British Columbia
www.ourfutureourpast.ca
www.basininstitute.org
www.imagescanada.org
www.whyte.org
www.glenbow.org

Authors Note:

The excerpts used in these stories are quoted from the original newspapers.

In some cases, the excerpt has been shortened, but all the spellings and the language remain original, only some typographical errors have been corrected for the sake of the reader.

References

Akrigg, G.P.V and Helen B. 1001 *B.C. Place Names*. Victoria: Sono Nis Press, 1986.

Beck, Janice Sanford. *No Ordinary Woman, The story of Mary Schäffer Warren*. Surrey:Rocky Mountain Books, 2006.

Dempsey, Hugh, ed. *The Best of Bob Edwards*. Edmonton: Hurtig, 1975.

Diehl, Fred. *A Gentleman from a Fading Age-Eric Lafferty Harvie* Devonion Foundation, 1989.

Graham, Clara. *Fur and Gold in the Kootenays*.Vancouver: Wrigley Printing Co. 1945.

Kaplan, Justin, ed. *Great Short Works of Mark Twain*. New York: Harper & Row, 1967.

Lees, J. A., and Clutterbuck, W. J. *A Ramble in British Columbia*. London: Longmans, Green & Co. 1888.

Luxton, Eleanor G. *Banff. Canada's First National Park*. Banff: Summerthought 1975.

Smyth, Fred J. *Tales of the Kootenays*. North Vancouver: J.J. Douglas, 1977.

Twain, Mark. *Who is Mark Twain*. Mark Twain Harper Studio, Mark Twain Foundation,University of California Press, 2009.

Warrender, Susan. *"Mr. Banff"The Story of Norman Luxton*. Calgary: Alistair Bear Enterprises, 2003

Photo Credits

Front Cover-View of Cascade Mountain, Banff National Park, Alberta (ca. late 1880s) Glenbow Archives (NA-2977-8)

Back Cover- Norman Luxton feeding his pet bear outside the Sign of the Goat Curio Store, ca. 1907), Whyte Museum of the Canadian Rockies. George Luxton,(Lux III B-Lux G)

Stereoscopic portraits of Norman Luxton 1905, Whyte Museum of the Canadian Rockies (Lux B 1-14)

Mary Schaffer on horse Whyte Museum of the Canadian Rockies (V527/PS-151)

Georgina Luxton, Hector Crawler, Norman Luxton, Mrs. Hector Crawler, at Banff Indian Days ca. 1915.)Whyte Museum of the Canadian Rockies, Byron Harmon, (V263/NA 3350).

Robert C. "Bob" Edwards, Calgary Alberta, ca. 1915 Glenbow Archives(NA-937-12)

Photo of Frederick J. Smyth from *The Cranbrook Herald* 1906

Photo of drawing of High Diving Elk from the *Moyie City Leader* circa 1900s

Photo of R.T. Lowery from the *Sandon Paystreak*, Sandon Historical Society

Photo of Sandon and caption from an original postcard, used with permission from Klaus Goedecke

Acknowledgements

I would like to thank the following organizations, associations and people who helped along the way.

Lena Goon and Elizabeth Kundert-Cameron for their assistance in the archives, at the Whyte Museum of the Canadian Rockies.

Michale Lang, Executive Director of the Whyte Museum of the Canadian Rockies, for permission to use excerpts from the excellent exhibition, The Stuff of Legend: The Luxton Family in Banff and the Bow Valley.

Brian Dees and Garry Anderson of the Canadian Museum of Rail Travel, for support and permission to use archival materials from the Cranbrook Historical Archives.

Tootie Gripich for her photographic skills, time and support in using the Family History Library

Susan Conrad for her comments and editorial support.

Katie Conrad for her support and enthusiasm.

Brian Clarkson and Bob Hutton, of Cranbrook Photo, for their expertise and assistance with photographic materials.

Jordan Osiowy for his computer savvy and technological support.

The Whyte Museum for permission to use archival photographs.

The Glenbow Archives for permission to use archival photographs.

Hugh Dempsey for giving me permission to quote excerpts from his book *The Best of Bob Edwards*.

Jim Hunter for the loan of the book, *Fur and Gold in the Kootenays*, by Clara Graham

Klaus Goedecke for permission to use his historical postcard of Sandon.

The New Denver Historical Association for archival materials.

Moyie High House Museum.

Barbara Stone and Bobby Dixon for their assistance and permission to view microfilms of the *Moyie Leader* newspapers.

Columbia Basin Trust and Columbia Kootenay Cultural Alliance for their financial contribution and support of this project.

Pauline Artifacet of the Cranbrook & District Arts Council.

And lastly, my first reader and editor, Brian Conrad.

Author Biography

Born in Montreal and graduated from McGill University with a B.A.

Has spent many years working in libraries, in the book trade, and as a contract researcher and freelance writer.

When not reading, writing or doing research, she spends her time gardening, doing upholstery, creating culinary delights, studying Spanish,dragonboating and looking for the next creative venture. *Rocky Mountain Tales* is her second book.

Photo by Tootie Gripich